THE **NIA** GUIDE FOR BLACK WOMEN
Balancing
Work and Life

Also by Sheryl Huggins and Cheryl Mayberry McKissack

The Nia Guide for Black Women:
Achieving Career Success on Your Terms

THE **NIA** GUIDE FOR BLACK WOMEN
Balancing
Work and Life

EDITED BY SHERYL HUGGINS
AND
CHERYL MAYBERRY MCKISSACK

AGATE

Chicago

Library of Congress Cataloging-in-Publication Data

The Nia guide for black women : balancing work and life / edited by Sheryl
Huggins & Cheryl Mayberry McKissack.
    p. cm.
    Summary: "Second in a series of empowerment guides for black women
developed by the editors and contributors to NiaOnline.com. Offers practical advice for balancing work and personal lives through tips, sugges-
tions, and personal stories from successful black women. Includes a list of
resources catering to working women of color"—Provided by publisher.
    ISBN 1-932841-05-9 (pbk.)
    1. African American women in the professions. 2. Career development.
3. Work and family. I. Huggins, Sheryl. II. McKissack, Cheryl Mayberry.

HD6054.2.U6N533 2005
650.1'082—dc22

2004025749

10 9 8 7 6 5 4 3 2 1

This book and all the books in *The Nia Guide for Black Women* series
are available in bulk at discount prices. For more information, go to
www.niaonline.com or agatepublishing.com.

Contents

DEDICATION

From Sheryl: To my family, for their loving support of my
balancing act

From Cheryl: To my nieces and nephews, Danielle, Ashley, Jessica,
Anthony, and Bobby, and my god-daughter, Kiara,
for teaching me the importance and value of balance

INTRODUCTION & ACKNOWLEDGEMENTS

When you were younger, did you dream that you could "have it all": a hot career, a busy social life, a loving family, *and* plenty of time left over to pursue hobbies, recreation, relaxation, and community outreach?

Now: how does that compare with your life today?

We thought so.

If you're like most of us, you're simply struggling to keep *any* kind of career going without alienating your loved ones and totally neglecting your health. Our lives are characterized by a constant string of deadlines and demands. Frequently, our happiness and personal well-being get lost in the shuffle. As black women, we have the added burdens of having to climb racial barriers, break glass ceilings, and live up to stereotypes such as the "Strong Black Woman." And we have less support from partners, given the higher rates of single motherhood and lower rates of marriage than the general U.S. population.

Truth is, we're far more likely to "have had it," than to "have it all."

In the first book of the ongoing *The Nia Guide for Black Women* series, we, the editors of NiaOnline (www.niaonline.com), focused on how you could "achieve career success on your terms." In this second book, we're focusing on the need to balance success at work with fulfillment at home, in the hopes of creating a more purposeful, integrated, well-rounded, and joyful life.

Ask yourself:
- Are you tired of playing superwoman?
- Would you like to get more support from your loved ones?
- Do you dare to follow your life's passion?
- Do you need help and resources for building your dream life?
- Are you ready to reinvent yourself?

These questions, and more, are addressed in the pages of this book. Since October 2000, as the web's premier resource for, by, and about black women and their families, NiaOnline has shared expert advice about balancing work and life, and finding your purpose (*nia* means "purpose" in Swahili). Through our annual Nia Enterprises Leadership Summit Series, we have connected the top sisters in their fields with women who are eager to succeed and grow. Through our online Consumer Advisory Panel (CAP), which reaches more than 100,000 black women and their families, we have been privy to the personal views of black women. In fact, each of the surveys included in this book are drawn from the results of an October 2004 online survey of 363 members of NiaOnline's CAP. *The Nia Guide for Black Women: Balancing Work and Life*, pulls all of this wisdom together. We hope you will enjoy reading it as much as we enjoyed putting it together.

The Nia Guide for Black Women: Balancing Work and Life is the latest leg of a journey begun by Cheryl Mayberry McKissack, who is the founder, president, and CEO of Nia Enterprises, LLC. In Chapter 13 of this book, "In Pursuit of Purpose," she shares the story of how starting the company helped her to balance work and life. Among the other personal stories of growth and purpose included here is that of Sheryl Huggins, who is editor-in-chief of NiaOnline and vice president of information services of Nia Enterprises (see hers in Chapter 10, "Having Time vs. Making Time").

Also contributing to the book and its elements are Nia Enterprises' vice president of sales and marketing, Heather Davis; vice president and chief technology office, Darcy Prather; office manager and assistant to the CEO, Yvette Shelby; and communications manager, Jessica Willis.

Our many thanks to the publisher of this book series, Doug Seibold, president of Agate Publishing in Chicago, as well as his staff. Project editor Patrick Lohier also deserves recognition for the many hours of work he put into *Balancing Work and Life*.

We also thank the editors, writers, and speakers who contributed to material from which this book is adapted, including, but not limited to Hilary Beard, Vonetta Booker-Brown, Carolyn M. Brown, Harriette Cole, Jeffrey Gardere, PhD, Reta J. Lewis, Shirley Moulton, Yvette Moyo, Lisa Price, Janice Cook Roberts, Teresa Ridley, Paula Sneed, Stephanie Stokes Oliver, Toby Thompkins, Monica Utsey, and Laura Washington.

Finally, we'd like to dedicate this book to our families, and their loving support of our balancing acts.

PART 1

ENDING THE

SUPERWOMAN SYNDROME

TIRED OF PLAYING
Superwoman?

Before you can balance work and life, you must escape the superwoman cape. Stephanie Stokes Oliver—who was NiaOnline's founding editor, remains a NiaOnline columnist, and is editor-in-chief of Essence.com— moderated a panel on the topic at the June 2003 Nia Enterprises Leadership Summit, held in Chicago. Below is her account of the advice shared by the participants.

"Show me a superwoman, and we'll show you a human being who's cranky, exhausted, and mentally and physically drained." That seemed to be the consensus of the "I'm Not Your Superwoman" panel of the June 2003 Nia Enterprises Leadership Summit, held in Chicago.

Moderated by Lorraine Cole, PhD, president and CEO of the Black Women's Health Imperative, and including panelists Hilda Hutcherson, MD, author of *What Your Mother Never Told You About S-E-X*; family therapist Marlene F. Watson, PhD, director of the graduate programs in couples and family therapy at MCP Hahnemann University; and me; the session was a rousing affirmation of the strength of black women.

It was also a definite testament to the fact that we can't "do it all"—and don't want to. We may not accept the superwoman mask, but we do like to consider ourselves to be Strong Black Women. So what's the difference? At bottom, the superwoman's a mythical sister. The "super" part of "superwoman" implies exceeding normalcy, or having superhuman capabilities.

In real life, that means not asking anyone for anything. In the comic books, did Superman or Wonder Woman ever ask for help? Nope; they were the saviors of everybody else. But it's hard to save everyone else if you can't save yourself.

Here are some particular superwoman stress points, and how our panelists addressed them.

Conjugal relations: Dr. Hutcherson mentioned that she once found herself in this pattern: After a long day at her medical practice, she would go home, prepare dinner, help her four children with homework, go back to work to finish paperwork, and then come home to find her husband ready for lovemaking.

Dr. Hutcherson's solution: At the burnout point, she called a family meeting and rallied the support of her loved ones to share more of the household duties. And it worked!

High anxiety: I had a similar breaking point. When I was thirty-six, I found myself overwhelmed at work and trying to be a supermom and superwife at home. I came to a screeching halt when I had an anxiety attack while hosting a party for my daughter's sixth birthday.

My solution: I decided that Saturdays would become my day

of rest. If God took a day off, who was I not to? I negotiated with my husband to have him do all the chauffeuring to and from our daughter's activities—even ballet class. As a result, he got so involved that he became head of the ballet school's parent association. In the spirit of reciprocation, I took over on Sundays—fully rested and recharged—while he performed couch potato duties watching the games on TV.

Is the Strong Black Woman image a negative or positive one?

Negative	12%
Positive	74%
Neutral	11%
I'm not sure	3%

Family backbone: At the panel, we discussed that if you are the person in your birth family who has reached the highest level of success, then there may be added burdens from family members who depend on you.

Dr. Watson's solution: She shared that she had persuaded a family member to seek counseling with her, to satisfying results. As a marriage and family counselor herself, she highly recommended such therapy; she also admonished black women for thinking that counseling is not for us, when it could give us an outlet for stress and an understanding ear.

Strategies for Strong Black Women

If you are strong enough to ask for help, then you can say you are a Strong Black Woman who shed the superwoman cape. Here are ways to get help:

- Everyone is overwhelmed, even our men. Before you get to the breaking point and approach a loved one in anger, think calmly of a way to get him or her to buy into a plan for sharing the burdens of housework and responsibility. That way, both of you win.

- Children are more capable than we often give them credit for. Kids can wash clothes by the time they are ten or eleven. By age twelve, children can learn to cook and be assigned cooking duties certain nights of the week.
- Trade a few hours of babysitting with another couple to establish a regular parents' night out. Offer to take care of a friend's children whenever she has a "mani-pedi" appointment, then drop yours off at her house when it's your turn.
- Send the kids to Mama for the summer the way black folks used to do. Give Mama a break in return that fits into your budget: a massage, a housecleaning, a plane ticket, etc.
- Let your mate know that foreplay may have been enough to turn you on when you weren't so overwhelmed, but now you need extra aphrodisiacs, such as weekend breakfasts in bed and dinners waiting when he gets home first. If you think that a man behind a vacuum cleaner looks sexy, let him know! Men may not do things as we would do them, but if your man gets the job done, let it go and get some rest!

Remember that this, too, shall pass. Nighttime infant feedings subside. Teenagers go off to college. Jobs change. You *can* have it all, just not all at the same time—thank goodness.

2

Are You Stressed
or **Blessed?**
TAKE OUR QUICKIE QUIZ

There's a popular saying in religious circles: "I am too blessed too be stressed." In truth, though, our God-given blessings—career, family, relationships—can sometimes send us to the edge of sanity and leave us praying for relief. For many women, our thirties and forties can be the most stressful times in our lives; in addition to developing our careers, we may be trying

What are your favorite ways to de-stress?			
Pray or meditate	44%	Eat favorite foods or go to a favorite restaurant	20%
Read a book	32%	Surf the internet*	19%
Go shopping	30%	Exercise or play a sport	17%
Sleep or vegetate	25%	Some other method	14%
Watch TV	23%	Party/socialize	7%
Make love	23%		

*All of the respondents are internet users

Each of the 363 respondents was able to choose two selections, so numbers add up to more than 100%.

to support a spouse, care for young children, and take care of elderly parents. Any one of these stressors can be challenging enough, but combinations of two or more can be brutal. When you're taking care of both younger and older members of your family, it puts you in what's called the "sandwich generation," the time of life when your stress levels might reach their peak.

However, stress is a part of everyone's life to one degree or another. Everyone has her own list of stress factors. But are you in charge of your stress, or is stress in charge of you? Take this ten-question quiz to find out.

The Nia Guide Stress Test

1. Between blessed and stressed, I more often feel:
   a. Stressed, definitely.
   b. About half and half.
   c. Truly blessed.

2. I exercise:
   a. Mostly by working out the remote control.
   b. Sometimes, when I can.
   c. Three or more times a week.

3. I eat:
   a. Whatever's quick, junk food or not—it's about speed.
   b. Fairly well most of the time, but slip sometimes when in a rush...
   c. Like my body is a temple and I am high priestess.

4. At work, when difficult people bother me:
   a. I give it to them full volume!
   b. I block them out.
   c. I take a breath, relax myself, then address the situation.

5. I last took a vacation:
    a. What's a vacation?
    b. Within the past twelve months.
    c. I just got back!

6. My love relationship is:
    a. Drama, 24/7.
    b. Marked by the same issues that affect every couple.
    c. Good and getting better.

7. I have ___ children under the age of twelve.
    a. Three or more.
    b. One or two.
    c. None.

8. In the last year, I have missed work:
    a. Frequently enough to raise eyebrows.
    b. A bit, but not more than the job allows.
    c. Not at all—I love being there!

9. I remain angry at people:
    a. Indefinitely.
    b. Long enough to see that they get what's coming to them.
    c. Grudges are a waste of energy.

10. My philosophy is:
    a. What goes around comes around.
    b. Life is what you make it.
    c. Don't worry; be happy.

Scoring: In order to prevent undue stress, this one was set up to make it easy for you. Obviously, this was a pretty informal quiz. If you answered mostly Cs, stress isn't bothering you. A majority of Bs means you deal with stress fairly well. If you got straight As, you are in need of a vacation and some major TLC!

3

WHO IS THE
Strong Black Woman?

With the raw strains of "Sisters Are Doing It for Themselves" as her theme song, she is the head of the household, the pillar of the community, and the wind beneath everybody's wings. She works full-time, cares for her family full-time, supports her man (if she as one) all the time, and whenever she feels her superhuman powers ebbing, she prays for strength and keeps on moving. Like generations of Strong Black Women before her, her steel-enforced back can bear any burden. Call on her if you need anything. Cross her or those she loves, and you may not survive her blistering wrath.

How long have you been trying to follow her lead? Probably for too long, according to Toby Thompkins, author of *The Real Lives of Strong Black Women: Transcending Myths, Reclaiming Joy*. "Strength has always been a defining character trait for black women....many sisters have been taught that suffering and self-sacrifice are key ingredients of a strong or 'good' woman," says Thompkins, who is a life coach and diversity consultant. "Too often, women of color feel compelled to become 'chronic caregivers,' sacrificing the ability to become truly free and fulfilled individuals," he adds. The myth of the Strong Black Woman exacts a great emotional and physical cost on its aspirants. Despite the nearly universal respect and deference it is given, the myth can be more limiting than it is empowering.

Below are the responses several NiaOnline.com members posted in response to Thompkins's work, many of them expressing relief to see in print what they already knew—that trying to live up to the Strong Black Woman image is self-defeating.

"I can totally relate, I am this Strong Black Woman,'" wrote C. Williams after reading the excerpt. "I was molested as a child, pregnant as a teen, then quickly married and divorced, with two more children. As a single mother I am 'doing it all'! Yet it doesn't all get done in a timely manner—or even effectively—because I am lonely and I sometimes need help. Everyone around says, 'You're doing a good job,' or 'Girl, keep your head up and it will all pay off in the end!' Blah, blah, blah. While other women all around me seem to be flourishing in relationships, men see me as being too independent or as if I don't need help, just sex! I don't know how to shake this cape, however, without falling from the sky! Help!"

Another woman saw the solution: "I am a former 'black superwoman.' I was unknowingly trained at an early age by my mother. Like most single black women, my mother had to work two jobs. The responsibilities of the home and my siblings were left to me. I was sexually abused by my mother's live-in boyfriend. I didn't tell her because he said it would hurt my mother and I had to take care of her. I carried this 'caretaker' role into adulthood. It wasn't until I tried to commit suicide, after struggling with issues relating to the sexual abuse, that I realized it was black superwoman who must die, and not me!"

Following are a few of Thompkins's observations about the Strong Black Woman ideal, and how all of us can escape the cape and live more fulfilled lives.

You call the role of the Strong Black Woman a myth—what exactly is this myth, and how did it come to be? What are the dangers of the myth?

The longest-standing myth about black women is that they are meant to be the pillars of strength in the American family. As the legendary nannies of so many white American families, and as the sole providers in so many of their own households, black women gave themselves over to the needs of others. During slavery, they birthed and nurtured new members into the slave labor pool, and the patriarchy quickly realized that controlling black women meant control of the race. Black women became strong in resistance to dehumanizing efforts to gain control over them. As the myth of the Strong Black Woman took hold in the American psyche, it denied black women the opportunity to create self-realized and personally fulfilling lives. Black women had no choice but to forsake opportunities to create lives of their own; today, the myth continues to threaten the Strong Black Woman's ability to embrace a deeper experience of love, self-care, sisterhood, and joy in her life.

What are the consequences for Strong Black Mothers and their children, especially their daughters, as this strength passes from one generation to the next?

As author and educator Jawanza Kunjufu once said, "Our mothers love their sons and raise their daughters." While both sons and daughters carve out their core identities by observing their parents, the Strong Black Woman archetype affects daughters more powerfully as the model they are expected to follow. They're imprinted with both the positive and negative aspects, often in ways they can't understand until later in their lives. Breaking free from the archetype is nearly impossible for some daughters.

The archetype—the myth—of the Strong Black Woman is unique to the black family; it drives all kinds of decisions that shape its character. Usually, the Strong Black Woman figure in the family, whether the mother, a grandmother, a big sister, or an aunt, sets the life expectations and rules for all the other members of the family, especially the young girls. They also create models of behavior for young boys. For example, when boys reach manhood, the early influence of the Strong Black Woman model can significantly affect how they behave toward women.

Many of the women I spoke to [for the book] said that while they felt compelled to live up to the example of a Strong Black Woman when they were young, they were equally driven to resist and reject much of it as they matured into adults. Rather than fighting the attribute of strength itself, they were struggling to free themselves from the guilt, denial, and self-sacrifice infused into this myth by American history. However, many Strong Black Mothers and their daughters have successfully developed honest, open, and supportive relationships as adults. Through my interviews, I have identified three key actions to assist in cultivating these healthy relationships: listen with a loving ear; live and let live; and develop compassion over blame.

A year before her passing, my mother had a near-death experience that dramatically changed her outlook on life. A lifelong Strong Black Woman, she realized that she had to let go of the day-to-day pain she dealt with every day for years in order to make peace with her own life before it was too late. I learned from her that to be truly happy in life, many risks would be necessary, and that sometimes there are things that you must let go. Her influence as Strong Black Woman throughout my life has shaped the way I behave toward others, especially women.

PART 2

GAINING SANITY
AND SUPPORT

4

INTERVIEW

Singer Brandy
on Quality Time

Motherhood has a way of changing everything about you. Just ask entertainer Brandy Norwood, whose journey to motherhood was captured on the 2002 reality show *Brandy: Special Delivery*. She says that even her thought processes changed after she became a mother, because she had to consider the needs of her daughter, Sy'rai, first.

Brandy spoke candidly about balancing motherhood and the demands of a superstar's performing schedule—as well as the source of her personal power—before the 2004 Intergenerational Celebration hosted in Washington DC by *Sister 2 Sister* magazine. (Hint: She has more than fame in common with Tom Cruise, John Travolta, and Isaac Hayes.)

The conversation was uniquely appropriate, since Brandy was at the annual gala to receive wisdom from a guiding elder, Donna DeBerry, executive vice president of diversity and corporate affairs for Wyndham Hotels—the highest-ranking woman and African American in the hotel industry.

Each September the Intergenerational Celebration pairs young black celebrities with older, high-profile mentors. "Our goal is to bridge the gap between the baby-boomer and hip-hop generations," says Jamie Foster Brown, publisher of *Sister 2 Sister*.

The conversation with the former star of TV's *Moesha* went deeper than the usual dishy details you can scrape off of any gossip rag. It didn't cover her engagement to L.A. Clippers basketball player Quentin Richardson or her eleven-carat engagement ring. Nor did it reveal any more details about her split from her daughter's father, Robert Smith, whom she is reported never to have legally married in the first place.

No, our dish is on an even more profound relationship in the twenty-five-year-old performer's life: the one she has with her two-and-a-half-year-old, Sy'rai.

What's the secret to your success in balancing being a new mom and a working woman?

I think it's just loving it all. The love of what you do motivates you to make sure you want to spend the quality time with your children and also work hard, do music, act, and things like that.

Especially when your children love what you do, it makes it a lot easier because you don't feel as bad [about not always being around]. Sy'rai loves to sing, she loves to dance, and she loves just being in my presence when I'm doing all of that. She is my biggest fan.

Do you feel pulled in different directions?

Oh yeah, I do, and I think you just have to learn how to say yes and how to say no.

Have you considered taking some extended time off to devote to Sy'rai full-time?

Well, when she was born, I didn't work at all. I stayed home for about a year. Then I got back into recording and singing when she was old enough to understand that this is what Mommy has to do. Of course, I take her with me. But she definitely understands that I have to go and perform and sing. That's how she became my biggest fan.

You practice Scientology. Is that your spiritual tradition?

No, I don't really have a spiritual tradition. My background is Christianity. I'm not a part of any type of religion, but that's [Scientology] a place where I go to get things off my chest, and it feels great. And I talk to my fiancé about everything, too.

What is the most important thing you know now as a mother, as opposed to when you were carrying Sy'rai?

Well, the thing is that I didn't think about what motherhood was going to be like. I know that sounds strange, but I made myself not think about it so that it could be a fresh experience and I wouldn't have any preconceived notions.

Of course, you have people who come in and tell you what it's going to be like, what you're going to have to do, what you're going to need, and what books to read. I just felt that way back in the day, people didn't have books to read and everybody telling them what to do with their children. So I just figured that if I followed my own instincts, then I would be okay, and that's what I did. It worked out pretty well for me. Of course, I made a lot of mistakes because I'm so young, but at the same time, I think mistakes are good because you get to learn from them and not make them again.

How do you feel about being a young mother?

It's very hard. I have a big life that I have to lead, and I want to still have a life of my own. Sometimes it's hard when you have a little baby that you have to look after; you want to make all the right decisions because whatever you do in your life will affect your children. When you don't have a child to think about, life is a lot easier; but when you do, the thought process is a little different.

Do you have any mothering mentors?
My mom is one. And I love some of the quotes that Jada Pinkett Smith has said about her children. That's pretty much it. Of course, I have my mothering rituals, mothering books, and stuff that I read.

I have this book called *A Cup of Comfort for Mothers and Daughters: Stories That Celebrate a Very Special Bond.* It talks about how the relationship between the mother and daughter is so strong, like no other relationship on earth, and you have to take the time and focus to be the best you can be, because you are an example to your children.

What was the best mothering advice you received?
I would have to say that [making room for] quality time is the most important. Your children can be around you all day, but if you don't spend quality time with them and you don't pay attention to them and talk to them and listen to them, it doesn't matter that they're just around you. Like, if I'm in dance rehearsal and I'm doing my thing, when we get a break, I go in the corner and talk to my daughter and kiss her and let her know that she's still important and it's not just all about what I'm doing over here.

And she's watching you?
Yeah, she's watching me, but if I never give her attention to let her know that *I know* she's watching, it doesn't matter as much.

5

SECRETS TO JOY

at **Work *and* at Home**

The old song goes, "I can bring home the bacon/Fry it up in a pan/And never, ever, ever let you forget you're a man."

Piece of cake—for the woman who doesn't need any sleep.

Trying to live up to that credo leaves most of us feeling like a piece of bacon frying on a skillet. Yet some women positively sizzle under such conditions, propelled by a clear life plan, plenty of confidence, and great organization skills. One of them is Paula Sneed, who is group vice president of Kraft Foods and president of e-commerce and marketing services for Kraft.

One of the highest-ranking black women in corporate America, Sneed is a member of Kraft's Management Committee, the company's fifteen-person policy decision-making group. Named to *Fortune* magazine's list of the "50 Most Powerful Black Executives," Sneed has also been recognized by *Black Enterprise*, *Ebony*, and *Working Mother*. She has been married to Lawrence

Bass for more than twenty-five years and raised a daughter, Courtney, who is in her twenties.

"A key to work, life, and success is recognizing what's really important," said Sneed on June 9, 2003, during the Nia Enterprises Leadership Summit in Chicago. There she participated in a news-style interview that was moderated by CNBC correspondent Sharon Epperson and included Deborah Sawyer, CEO of Environmental Design International Inc. Here is some of the advice that Sneed shared that day for balancing a successful work life with a fulfilling family life.

Have a Life Plan

"All through my life—even today—I have had both what I would call a short-term plan and a long-term plan. One thing I did in business school, which I would suggest for all of you, came out of a course I took called 'Self-Assessment and Creative Development,' and it was this fabulous course [in which] you spent a semester figuring out who you were and what that meant for your career long-term.

"One of the exercises was to draw a picture of what your life was like at that moment. I was a second-year business student, and any of you who remember what it was like being in school knows that your life is sort of in disarray. I had dollar signs with zeros next to [them]; I had all of these things that signified chaos... Then they said, 'Draw a picture of what you want your life to be like in ten years,' and so I drew another picture, and then they said, 'Now take the two pictures and put them side by side and think through what are the bridges between the two pictures—and that's your game plan.' That's your personal game plan and your professional game plan.

"That exercise was incredible for me because it really did

demonstrate very visually what my life was like and what I wanted it to be like. My picture in ten years included a husband and a job and a little community service, and it had a couple of children in the picture. So I drew exactly what I wanted my life to be like and then it gave me a road map...and I used that so many times.

"My husband and I always have a game plan [now] be-cause...even if you should decide a couple of years into the plan that you don't want to do it—like I did every few years, changing from teaching to social work to whatever—the game plan gives you motivation around getting up every day and fo-cusing and accomplishing, so you can get to points that are dif-ferent from where you are today.

"When I did my first plan...I could be very selfish because it only included me, but then when I met my husband [Lawrence] right as I was getting out of school...we had to develop a mutual plan...because there was going to be some compromise that each of us had to make to accommodate the grand plan for both of us.

"If you don't have this life plan, every interruption that comes along, or everything that seems to be disruptive, is a problem, but if you've got a life plan—if you're figuring out how you're managing all of these things—it doesn't make it any more or less annoying, but it does make it less disruptive."

Pick the Right Partner

"I also think it's really important to pick the right partner. I have been very fortunate: I've been married for twenty-five years, and I didn't get married until I was thirty, so I sort of got rid of all the people I shouldn't have married, and I didn't marry in my twenties. So when I found my husband, I sort of knew what I was looking for: someone who was going to love me when I was fat and fifty, and be a great provider and all that.

"I really found somebody that I thought would be a great father, a great husband over the longer term, and once I picked that person, I recognized [he had those qualities] because my parents were married fifty years before my dad died. The key to a long marriage is good communication, because we think people can read our minds, and they can't."

Ask for the Order

"Just like we have to ask for the order from our business environment, we have to ask for the order [from] our spouses. Many times, women take on too much. Like I was taking on... when we had our daughter [Courtney]. I was thinking I had to do everything. [Then] I thought, 'Wait; he could take care of our daughter.' He's an engineer; he would love to see her teeth move.' I find that experience uninteresting.

"We divided the work up, we communicated with each other about stuff...I used to think I had to stop and get the milk even though we had live-in help, but then I thought, 'Give this man [Lawrence] a list,' and I always tell young women, 'Communicate with your spouse. Tell men what you want them to do. Give them a list; they'll respond.'

"They like lists, you know, but if you think they're going to go to the refrigerator and see there's no milk and stop on the way home, it doesn't happen. They never do! They'll drink the last bit of the milk and throw it in the trashcan and still realize there's no milk because—you know why? We will go there and get it...I always say to young women, 'Have you given your husband a list?' They go, 'No.' 'Have you told your husband [you] really want to work for this job?' The communication and dividing the work becomes important.

"Women tend not to want to be pushy, particularly African American women of my generation. We were taught, 'Don't be pushy. People don't like rude and pushy people.' There is a difference between being pushy and being persistent and persuasive and asking for the order, whether it's in my relationship with my child (I don't have to ask, I *demand* the order, or at least I used to; now she is twenty-two, and it is a little bit different); in a relationship where we sit down and talk about what's important and what we want in the near term or the long term; or at work on the boards that I am on.

"I really always decide what it is I want, or what it is that I am going after, and then I make it clear to people in ways that hopefully aren't offensive that this is what I am interested in. I think we have to learn it and practice it, because sometimes when we're not used to it, it sounds aggressive and threatening. If we sound aggressive and threatening, we don't get what we want. Asking for the order can be done very pleasantly, very affirmatively, but very firmly, and it really helps to clarify for people what it is that's important to us and what we need to continue on our pathway for success."

Invest in the Things that Matter

"Invest in childcare. I drove a ten-year-old Honda even when I was a VP because I was paying my babysitter more money than the Lord will allow, and I knew if I was going to have a person who was in my home co-mothering with me—to help me raise a successful, healthy, intelligent child—I really [couldn't] scrimp on childcare. I can scrimp on the Honda. My administrator had a better car than me, but I recognized that my number-one investment every month, beyond investing in our future for retirement, was investing in childcare.

"We had only three bedrooms at one point, and the babysitter was living down the hall, and it really did crimp our love style during the week until the babysitter went home on the weekend. But the reality was, every morning I [could] get up, get my clothes on, and go to work, and every night I came home to a clean house and the dinner was cooked. It made a difference in my life because I didn't have to worry about dry-cleaning, etc.

"Now, I tell ya, when my daughter went away to school, I had to do my own dry-cleaning, and oh my God! I had to do things I just didn't recognize. All of a sudden I had to give my husband a new list, you know, because now we [didn't] have a lot of the help we had before... We oftentimes think we can't afford certain stuff, but I didn't get manicures; I didn't get a lot of the stuff that I would have liked to have gotten because my priority was making my life simple in one dimension."

Love Each Other's Dreams

"Love your partner's dreams. Your partners all have dreams. If you want them to love your dream and respect it and help you get it, you have to love theirs. One time I worked on a project all summer long, and I worked like a dog on this project, invested so many hours. I literally gave up our summer for this project.

"The day I was supposed to present it to the president of the company, I was definitely ill. I was throwing up all night. I woke up in the morning—I was so sick—and I said to my husband, 'I can't go to work today,' and he goes, 'Isn't this the day you're presenting that project?' I said, 'Yeah.' He said, 'No, no, you're going to work today.' He said, 'Go take a shower. I am driving you to work. I'm going to call my client and tell them I'll be there this afternoon.'

"He drove me to work and I presented. We got the funding for the project. I came right out of the meeting—my boss knew I was deathly ill—got right in the car, went back home. [My husband] said, 'You want this so badly, it's going to make the difference if you get promoted on time or late.' He understood the dimension of this project.

"He loved my dreams well enough to do whatever it took to achieve my dream, and comparably, I loved his dream. He has his own company, and I always wanted somebody to pay me every two weeks. You know, I get the check, it gets deposited in the bank. He is an entrepreneur, and so in the beginning I didn't understand entrepreneurship (though I learned to love entrepreneurship)—just like he didn't understand why anybody would want to put up with corporate nonsense."

Recognize What's Important

"My mom said to me when I got married, 'You'll recognize when you're seventy, when you have a good marriage and you got children that love you, that's what's important,' because no one will ever remember what was on your business card in 1995. I can't even remember what was on my business card in 1995. She said, 'What's important is the closest people to you. Never forget it.'

"Having that consistently in front of my mind—no matter what I had been going for professionally—has really made a difference in my life, because at the end of the day, when I talk to my daughter or my husband, I realize how good my life is. It is not about coming out of a meeting and feeling like I accomplished something. That is just a part of being comfortable and having resources, but what's really important is knowing that after twenty-five years, I am still in a good relationship.

"One of the happiest days of my life was when my daughter got her degree, last Thursday. I just felt like I was an accomplished person. All this other stuff is interesting, but the fact that I was—in these difficult times—able to raise a healthy African American female child is a good thing. To me that's what life-and-work balance is all about."

6

SURVIVAL STRATEGIES
for the Stressed-Out Working Mom

Teresa Price, an educational consultant who works from home, sat down one afternoon and made a list of all the things she does for her family. After writing down item number twenty, she couldn't believe how she had been able to juggle everything from driving her two sons back and forth to school in Bethesda (about thirty minutes from her DC home), delivering food to the needy, and volunteering on several boards, to managing the sports schedule of two very active boys and putting in a thirty-hour work week. When Price, who is married, was rushed to the hospital for emergency surgery for an inguinal hernia (a condition in which abdominal soft tissue protrudes through a weak point in the groin), she knew she had to make some changes.

"Now I have quiet time in the morning and do prayer and meditation. I take time out to do things by myself for fun. I also got involved with a carpool, which helped tremendously," Price said.

De-stressing required Price to rearrange her life and priorities. "I completed things that I put off, like having our hard-
wood floors refinished, the bathroom redone, and other home
improvements. I learned how to delegate responsibilities and
had some bodywork done for myself, such as reflexology and
massage. I'm doing more yoga. I'm feeling more relaxed. I'm
working at not responding and reacting to things that press my
buttons and pull my triggers. I'm trying to establish more balance in my life," Price said.

What exactly is stress and how does it affect the body? When
we are faced with a dangerous situation, our body is sent a 911
signal and every organ responds. This is the fight-or-flight response. The physiological changes our body experiences as a
result of immediate stress include the rush of adrenaline and
cortisol (the stress hormones) into our bloodstream; the ele-
vation of our heart rate and blood pressure; our saliva drying up
and the digestion and elimination systems stopping so blood
can be directed away from our internal organs to our muscles
and brain; and, the most dangerous of all, the immune system's efficiency declines.

This response is necessary if we are facing harm, but chronic
stress—the kind that never seems to let up—keeps the body in a
constant state of terror. According to the National Institute for
Occupational Safety and Health, when the body is repeatedly
subjected to false alarms, it becomes worn down and our biologi-
cal systems are damaged, inhibiting the body's ability to heal.
As a result, our bodies become ripe for cardiovascular disease,
musculoskeletal disorders, and psychological disorders.

It's no surprise that the daily demands of staying on top of a
career while taking care of a family can create chronic stress—
especially if you feel as if you're failing to keep up. Chronic
stress can be the result of an unhappy marriage or relationship,

an overly demanding job, a dysfunctional family situation, or all of the above. Childhood trauma and a negative worldview can also be sources of continual stress for some women.

There are several different types of warning signs for stress. While each of them can have other causes besides stress, if you are experiencing them you should consider the possibility that you are stressed out.

Emotional Warning Signs
- Anxiety
- Sleep disruption
- Anger
- Inability to concentrate
- Unproductive worry
- Sadness
- Frequent mood swings

Physical Warning Signs
- Stooped posture
- Sweaty palms
- Chronic fatigue
- Weight gain or loss
- Infertility
- Physical symptoms that your doctor cannot attribute to another condition

Behavioral Warning Signs
- Overreacting
- Acting on impulse
- Using alcohol or drugs
- Withdrawing from relationships
- Changing jobs often
- Feeling agitated most of the time

Alena Henry, a single mother and administrative assistant who lives in Laurel, Maryland, almost reached a breaking point before recognizing the warning signs of chronic stress in her life.

"I was working full-time, going to school full-time, and taking care of a child under the age of one," Henry said. "I was feeling overwhelmed and stressed to the point where I wanted to get in my car, and drive away leaving everyone behind. I had to stop and make some adjustments."

Now Henry works part-time, attends college part-time, and has joined a mothers' support group where she can call upon more than eighty women for support.

How often do you feel "stressed out"?	
At least once a week	39%
Daily	28%
At least once a month	20%
Rarely	12%
Never	1%

De-stressing can go beyond changing your routine or scaling back your commitments. Often it starts in the mind, as Pam Jackson, a single mother who works for the Library of Congress in Washington DC has learned. "Whenever I ask for help, I feel like I am imposing on people and inconveniencing people," Jackson said. She had to learn to rely more on her father and brother to help her care for her son, she said. Reaching out to her extended family, simplifying her life, and learning to forgive her ex-husband have helped Jackson to cope more with stress. "I streamline, streamline, streamline...my spending, my time, my household chores, everything. I keep it simple, do only what is necessary, spend on only what is necessary, and sacrifice now because wealth and prosperity are coming," Jackson said. "And I've trained myself to forgive and forget."

While stress can be very complicated, relieving stress need not be. According to the National Women's Health Information

Center of the U.S. Department of Health and Human Services, handling stress can be addressed by doing simple things, such as a regular routine of relaxation techniques that can include deep breathing, yoga, meditation, or massage therapy; making time for yourself to do things you enjoy, such as taking a bubble bath; getting adequate sleep and exercise; and, eating a healthy diet.

Avoiding processed foods and foods that cause stress on the system, such as artificial sweeteners, soft drinks, chocolate, eggs, fried foods, junk foods, white flour, and caffeine is paramount, according to Dr. James Balch and his wife, nutritionist Phyllis A. Balch, authors of the *Prescription for Nutritional Healing*. They also recommend anti-stress herbs such as catnip, chamomile, kava kava, and Siberian ginseng.

However, sometimes the symptoms related to stress point to a more serious medical or emotional problem. Therefore, no stress reduction plan is complete without a trip to your doctor to rule out or address such problems.

7

WHEN MOMMY
needs a Time-Out

"Time-outs" aren't only for kids, anymore. Here, journalist Stephanie Stokes Oliver shares her personal story of how she has been able to carve out "me" time from a busy schedule as mother, wife, and top editor.

I once read a delightful magazine story about a woman with many children who relished her annual Mothers Day gift from her family: a pampering weekend alone.

Every year, on the Friday before Mothers Day, her husband and children would drive her to her favorite hotel within a few hours of her home. After she checked in, the kids got to see her hotel room, jump on the single bed, ride down the glass elevator—and scamper right back to the car to go home.

Then this woman would begin her three days of solitude, full of books, massages, room service, TV, movies —whatever. On

Sunday evening her family would return to find a cheerful, re-freshed mom to take to a fine Mothers Day dinner.

I found it interesting that the story was told by the woman's now-adult daughter. So not only had the mother reaped the benefit of her annual weekend break from parenting, but she also had passed along the joy and importance of this new tra-dition to her daughter.

As a mom myself for more than nineteen years, I've estab-lished some time-out methods too. Here are a few—some of them tongue-in-cheek—that might work for you. And best of all, they're effective any day of the year.

- Name your child after your mother. (It's a great way to get all the babysitting you want.) I know a Chicago woman who actually used this tactic successfully.
- Sleep when the baby sleeps. It's almost cliché, but it bears repeating. When we have an infant who sleeps sporadically, we're tempted to use the time to clean up, run an errand, or make a call. But if you can grab some rest when the baby conks out, you'll feel as if you had a quick time-out. I got this tip honestly: recently, after her newborn fell asleep in his swing, a friend called to cancel our impending lunch together so she could take a much-needed nap.
- Make a particular day of the week "Daddy Day." Hype it as a special day for when your child's father is responsible for her or his total care. If you're a single mother, establish a routine schedule of weekends and holidays when Dad has custody. This can provide you with blocks of time that you can plan on. A divorced woman in New Jersey, who has primary custody of her son, tells me that her child's Daddy Days provide "the true joy of single motherhood." Her ex

is a good father who wants to have their son with him as often as possible—and that's cool with her.

- Cultivate relationships with other mothers of children your child's age to trade off babysitting. When it's your turn without the kids, use the time to go where you're not likely to see children, or stay home to relax, regroup, refresh.

- Give your child a summer sabbatical—from you. By the time your child is around six years of age, you can send him or her on airplanes unaccompanied, under the care of the airlines. It's an old African American tradition to send children "down south" to Grandma. My mother lives "out west" in Seattle and was gracious enough to offer to keep my daughter every summer. The bonding between grandparents and children is precious, and the time you can take to get reacquainted with your child's father—or yourself—is priceless. If your mom lives near you (or in your house) or has made it clear that she finished with childcare after she finished raising *you*, send Junior to another loving relative or to a sleep-away camp (the educational value will help you feel less guilty).

Can't bear to be away from the kids but still need a break? Go on vacation with your children at resorts that cater to families—not just to kids. These vacation spots have activities for adults and separate ones for children. Some even have babysitting included in the package. I have done this and found that you can be on vacation together and not see your children all day, and everybody's actually happy about it. My faves: Club Med in Eleuthera, Bahamas (moderately priced for an all-inclusive); Franklyn D. Resort in Jamaica (intimately-sized resort with townhouse-like accommodations); Beaches in Jamaica; and Turks & Caicos (pricey, but the best).

8

WORK WISELY:

Get Organized!

A crucial step to balancing work and life is staying organized. Here, Harriette Cole—who juggles being a mother, wife, life coach, syndicated etiquette colum- nist, author, and NiaOnline columnist—shares her story of how she got it together.

I often joke with people about my organizational skills. In nearly every other area of physical life, I can be masterful. When it comes to where I put my stuff, however, I fail miserably.

This has been a chronic problem for me—one that I have learned that I share with a lot of people. Creating a place for something and making sure that it ends up there—every time—just doesn't seem to happen for a whole lot of folks. As a result, the unlucky ones end up losing their jobs, misplacing their receipts, forgetting an important deadline, or otherwise messing up. Why? Because their space is a mess.

In preparation for 2003, I decided that I wanted to start afresh. My yearly plans to get organized had failed in the past. Even with the best of intentions, I had somehow consistently fallen short of my goal of organizing *all* of my papers and things and keeping them that way. A new project, deadline, or other pressing business distraction inevitably got in the way, leaving me and my stuff bound to my old ways.

Enter the savior of my office, a sister with a nose for order that dares you to get in the way. Jen Doman, founder and president of Get It Together: Home, Office & Estate Organization in Brooklyn, New York, practices what she preaches. She is a woman who spent years helping other people get their personal and work lives in order (just because she was good at it and she liked them) has now turned her savvy into a business.

I enlisted her support at the end of last year so that I could do what I've been threatening to do for years: make my workspace neat and fully functional. I am elated to report that my small space, which produces a huge volume of work through a number of dedicated employees, now matches the image I want to project. Jen is responsible.

Following are some pointers I gleaned from working with Jen. They may help you get your office, cubicle, or desk organized so that you can start the year off right.

- **Declare your intention to get your workspace neat and organized.** Be very clear with yourself about what you want to accomplish. Write a list outlining each task that must be fulfilled—from emptying your desk drawers to reorganizing your filing cabinet. Don't consider any task too small to list.

- **Make a timeline and check off your list against it.** Be specific about what must be done, and give yourself dates by which each item will be completed. Check off each completed duty and mark the date it was finished next to it. Over time you will see your progress, even if some things don't quite happen on time.

- **Pick a day of the week to handle the tough stuff.** According to Jen, "Everyone has a day of the week they like the least (most people say Monday). Use that day to go through just one stack of papers. You don't have to move mountains—but molehills, you can do! Initially spend no more than thirty minutes going through these items, deciding what should be filed and what should be tossed. After a few thirty-minute sessions, start spending *one* hour of *one* day going through *one* stack. This is very manageable. Once you've decided what you need to keep, create some type of graded system. You can do this with small boxes or organizational items that can be ordered from office-supply stores. The idea is to keep your filing method confined to small spaces. How much can you really fit into a small box? Not much! Large, open areas are a nightmare for those who are organizationally challenged. It gives them license to continually spread their possessions everywhere. Tight slots and spaces will force you to be organized. Additionally, as you aspire for that promotion, keep in mind that your employers will want to know that you are organized. Your desk should *never* be messier than your boss's desk."

- **Seek out help if you need it.** Just because you're good at one thing doesn't mean you're good at another. If you've already proved to yourself that you need support in getting the job done, identify a professional to help you now. And don't be embarrassed about your decision. Pretending that you will improve next year, or that things aren't as disorganized as you think (when deep down you know they are), is delusional. Be wise and take charge of this key area of your work life. As Jen explains, "A professional organizer can consult with you to find out what organizational systems are preferable and realistic to you. As an example, an elaborate color-coded system for filing and remembering dates and documents can be developed. After helping you put a system in place, a professional organizer will stay in touch with you to make sure that you are not falling down on the organizational job. Organizing is not just about getting the clutter off of your desk. The art of organizing is about helping you create mental and physical space so that you can become more efficient and productive. A professional organizer will spend time with you to help you understand why the clutter keeps showing up on your desk and in your office space. If you don't understand the why of it, you won't be able to control it, and instead it will always control you."

- **Stay on top of your space.** After you have systems in place, reserve a time each day for keeping it operational. A few minutes a day can mean the difference between a well-organized workspace that lasts only through January and one that remains so come July.

9

A MAN'S ADVICE FOR

Getting Support
from **Your Partner**

Why should you struggle alone to balance work and life? Sometimes you need your mate's support. Here, clinical psychologist, author, and NiaOnline columnist Jeff Gardere, PhD, shares his perspective on the topic, as a relationship counselor, and as a man.

In a September 2004 *New York Times* article, writer Edmund Andrews reviewed a survey conducted by the Department of Labor which showed that the average working woman spends about twice as much time as the average working man on household chores and the care of children. The average working woman, for example, spends about one and a half hours a day caring for other members of the family and one hour and twenty minutes on household chores, while the average working man spends barely fifty minutes caring for family members and less than forty-five minutes on household chores. In addition, almost as many women as men hold jobs—about 78 percent of women, compared with 85 percent of men. Andrews's conclusion, quite simply, is that working women out-juggle men, when it comes to keeping a career going and keeping the home fires burning. Something we always knew, but could never be proven, until now.

But as obvious as it is that working women wear many hats, many men have been in denial about the disparity, and therefore eerily quiet. Many men still have misogynistic views that lead them to believe that as long as they have a job, make money and pay the bills, their female partner—whether she is working or not—should carry the extra burden of doing household chores and raising children. Such men see themselves as being exempt from "women's work," because real men don't do laundry, or make dinner for the kids, or change diapers. They believe that as long as a man is gainfully employed, he has fulfilled his responsibilities as husband and father.

On the other hand, poor Mary has to be a superwoman. She has to run the office, come home, run after the kids, and then after her exhausting day, she still must run around the bed a few times doing her fertility dance so that he will reward her with some real loving! And if she cannot keep a perfect home every single day, or she asks him to microwave some leftovers, he calls her lazy! To add insult to injury—and I know the guys are going to get ticked off that I am letting this dirty little secret out—many men opt to work later in order to avoid the chaos of early evening family life, which includes chores and helping the kids with homework.

Now, as the DOL numbers suggest, there are men who contribute to the running of the household and support their wives in the juggling of family and work. And let me be clear here:

this isn't about the good guys who help versus the bad guys who don't. Many of the guys who don't help out at home are not being vindictive; this simply is the way they were raised by their fathers *and* mothers. They were taught by words and deeds that daddy works outside of the home, while mama works at home and outside, too!

Plus, there's the overcompensating attitude of some women, who do not trust their men to help out around the house, other than cutting grass and emptying out the garbage! They think we men are just plain inept when it comes to housekeeping. In my household, for example, my wife will not allow me to do dishes, because she claims I do not wash them well enough. Now tell me, what's wrong with putting some soap on the dish, and then just rinsing it off with cold water instead of hot? (Don't answer all at once!) The point is some women discourage us from helping out because they do not trust our competence, so they do everything themselves.

Given these facts, the $64,000 question becomes: How can working women convince their men to take on more of the burden of caring for the home and children? Here are some strategies that have worked for couples I have assisted as a psychologist and relationship counselor:

- **Let's start from the very beginning.** We must stop raising our boys and girls to believe that there is such a thing as women's work. Instead they should be taught by words and deeds that the family is a unit and everyone must contribute in whatever way it takes to get all of the work done. Dads can do a little more housework, as well as spending more time with the kids when they get home from work. Seeing this, our kids will emulate these same behaviors as they grow to adulthood.

- **For heaven's sake, let your men help!** Don't be an over-compensating mama. Okay, so they may burn the food, or wax the floor with a dirty mop. Don't denigrate your men. Praise and encourage them verbally (even if you think they are domestically challenged) and show them how to do it better! Don't be afraid to let them change diapers and bathe the kids. Remember, practice makes perfect! In counseling, I have instructed some couples to make it dad's job to spend at least one hour playing with the kids and then preparing them for bed, so mom can kick back and smoke a cigar, belt some scotch, and read the newspaper. (Okay, forget the cigar.)

- **Set up a weekly schedule together that divides up the household chores.** One night you clean the dishes; the next night it's his turn. As career women, you can't run home by six o'clock every night, or you will never move up the ladder. Instead work out an arrangement allowing you to work late some nights. On those nights he will be responsible for the household until you get home. He should also have dinner waiting (microwaveable food and takeout are allowed)! If he does a decent job, then you can reward him by letting *him* run around the bed a few times doing his fertility dance to get you in the mood!

- **Run the numbers and show him how much your time is really worth.** Actually make up a spreadsheet showing him what it would cost to pay full-time help to do all the household chores, tutoring, homework babysitting, etc. Or otherwise, lay out what it would cost for you to give up your job in order to take care of the home front full-time. That should get his attention, and quickly.

- **Finally, just talk.** Stop sitting on your feelings, suffering and seething in silence. He will not "get it" if you don't let him know that there is a real problem. Talk to one another about the importance of your work as a career woman, partner, and mother. If he is half the man you thought he was or could be when you hooked up with him, eventually he will have the humanity and compassion to understand you and do more to accommodate your ambitions.

PART 3

FINDING YOUR FOCUS AND
FOLLOWING YOUR PASSION

10

Having Time
VS.
Making Time

How you prioritize is crucial to achieving balance between work and life. Here, Sheryl Huggins, who is NiaOnline's editor-in-chief and one of this book's editors, shares her philosophy on how to establish those priorities.

If you're like me, you really don't have the time to give yourself the attention and tender loving care you deserve. If you're like me, you also make the time for it anyway.

Truth is, at any given moment, there's some task or chore I could be doing, some obligation I could fulfill. As the editor-in-chief of NiaOnline, there's always one more article I could be editing, another interview to transcribe, or a phone call I should have returned at least a week ago. As a new condo owner in Brooklyn, there always seems something that needs fixing or improving. Meanwhile, the number of unopened emails in my inbox multiplies, and the ever-growing stack of bills and junk mail on my living room coffee table threatens to topple over. I only wish I would go through the mail nightly, like I should. I could tackle all of those tasks, and still have plenty more to do.

But rarely does a week go by when I don't enjoy a four-mile run in Brooklyn's oasis, Prospect Park. With tunes loaded on my MP3 player, I literally run down memory lane with Al Green, Stevie Wonder, and Earth, Wind and Fire as my own private soundtrack. Never mind the aches or twinges that grow more frequent each year; my heart is pumping, my legs stretch out to take each new step, and during that time I feel *so* alive. As someone who had already suffered both gall bladder disease and high blood pressure by my early thirties, I see this as a way to chase down the good health I deserve. My blood pressure is down, and the stomach aches are kept at bay. Chores can wait! I may not have the time for this, but I'll "make" the time.

See, I don't believe in the concept of "having time" for something. Most sisters are juggling too many balls in the air—label them family, love life, career, community—to "have the time" for anything. When you've got more responsibilities than time, the only way out is through prioritizing. It's something we do constantly, though we're rarely aware of it. We simply make the time for those things that matter most to us.

When it's ten p.m. and you're still in the office instead of at home with your partner, it's because you've decided that at the moment, working takes priority over your time with him. When you skip your morning yoga class for the third week in a row because you really need that extra forty-five minutes of shuteye before you start your busy day, at that moment sleep has taken priority over exercise. You can say you didn't have

Which of the following things are you mostly likely to sacrifice in your daily routine?

Exercise	52%
Housework/chores	42%
Good nutrition	30%
Socializing	24%
Sleep	22%
Love/sex life	17%
Grooming/appearance	10%
Family time	6%
Career/work	4%

Selections ranked in descending order of the percentage of total respondents who chose them. Each of the 363 respondents was able to choose two selections, so the poll totals add up to more than 100%.

the time for yoga, but the truth is you decided to make time for a little more sleep.

Recently, NiaOnline asked more than 360 black women which things they are most likely to sacrifice during their daily routine. At the top of the list were exercise (52 percent), housework/chores (42 percent), and good nutrition (30 percent). (See the chart on this page for the other responses.)

Okay, it's not exactly a newsflash that there are a plenty of out-of-shape, fast-food-eating sisters with messy homes (come on, you know who you are). So I decided to turn the list upside down, and look at what they were *least* likely to say they would sacrifice. After all, that tells you what is valued the most. The results, from the bottom up: career/work (4%), family time (6%) and grooming/appearance (10%). In other words, there *are* plenty of fly-looking sisters who take care of business at work and in the family circle ("big up" to you ladies, you know who you are too.)

What those results also suggested is that self-care (exercise, nutrition) is at the bottom of the priority list, and taking care of others (children, partners, the boss) is at the top.

National health statistics reflect the damage caused by putting self-care last. More black women (15 percent) are likely to say they're in fair or poor health than white women (11 percent), according to the Centers for Disease Control and Prevention. More than *three-quarters* of African American women between the ages of twenty and seventy-four are at least overweight, and half are obese (weighing 20 percent or more over their ideal body weight), compared to over half (58 percent) of white women being at least overweight and 31 percent being obese (National Institutes of Health, 2000). Heart disease, diabetes, high blood pressure, respiratory disorders, arthritis, and some cancers are all ailments for which being obese puts you at risk.

Furthermore, black women have higher mortality rates from heart disease, stroke, and most cancers than white women. In fact, as of 2001, black women's average lifespans were five full years shorter than white women's (seventy-five years and eighty years, respectively).

But what's a few less years to us when we know we're looking so fly?

Seriously, as you juggle all of life's balls, make taking care of yourself as high a priority as the time you spend at the office or for your weekly "press and curl." After all, you're no good to your employer when you're sick, and you sure aren't any good to your loved ones when you're six feet under—no matter how good you look.

That's why I do make time for at least one four-mile run a week, and I've made healthy eating a priority. Both efforts make me feel better, and give me more energy to keep the other balls in the air.

On the other hand, my eyebrows are long overdue for a tweezing…where did the time go?

TAKE NOTE:

Are you having a tough time making yourself a priority among the many items on your weekly to-do list?

Use the space below to list everything you've been meaning to do within the next week, even if you don't think you'll possibly have the time to get to them. Now go back and rank them in order of importance or urgency. Take the top five items, and list them in a separate "must-do" list. Then pick a sixth item from the bottom of your ranked list—the more fun and self-indulgent, the better—and add that to your must-do list for the week. Whatever you do during the next week, make sure you check off all six must-do's. Good luck, and take care.

_____

_____

_____

_____

_____

_____

_____

_____

_____

_____

_____

_____

_____

_____

_____

_____

_____

_____

_____

_____

_____

_____

_____

_____

_____

_____

_____

_____

_____

_____

_____

_____

_____

11

Are You **Passionate About Your Career?**

YOU SHOULD BE

Let's face facts: many adults still don't know what we want to be when we grow up. We do work that we find mundane and meaningless. We get up grudgingly every Monday morning and immediately start the countdown to Friday.

According to a Gallup poll, only 39 percent of U.S. workers are completely happy with their jobs. Even among the self-employed, fewer than 60 percent report being satisfied with what they're doing. That leaves a lot of unhappy wage earners out there singing, "Got me working, working, day and night."

Unless you were born independently wealthy or married someone who is, recently hit a multimillion-dollar lottery jackpot, or invested in the stock market at an early age, you accept that you will have to work most of your life to support yourself, and—if you fit into the majority of black women—your family.

Since you will be on the payroll for forty or more years, it makes sense to try to make a living doing something you love—

or at least really like to do. What doesn't make sense is going through years of school or training and working long hours in a career for which you have no intrinsic interest, just because it offers external rewards such as prestige and high pay. Ultimately, those external rewards are unlikely to make up for a lack of internal benefits like peace of mind and personal contentment.

There *is* a way to pursue work that not only pays the bills but also nurtures your spirit. Here are some ideas to get you started:

- **Put what you enjoy doing first, and what you are good at second.** Pursuing your passion is about more than just finding what you are good at. Aptitude tests and experiences will tell you what you can do, but you have to search deep within to find what you will be happiest doing.

- **Make your career fit your lifestyle, not the other way around.** First you must learn to separate what you do for a living from who you are. If you work better from home, then seek out opportunities to work at home for at least part of the week.

- **Focus on what you *don't* want and what you *do* want.** Write down what your ideal life would look like. Search the past for present-day passion. Make a list of activities and subjects that grabbed your attention as a child. Why did they hold your interest? Once you know what you want, look at how you might make it happen. Itemize the steps in your plan of action.

- **Think outside the box by experimenting.** Don't stay confined to your day-to-day life—explore something totally new. Consider signing up for a class on gourmet cooking, creative writing, or public speaking. If you like to talk nonstop and don't want to be stuck in a nine-to-five routine, think of ways to represent your company outside of the office, such as giving talks at colleges or workshops.

- **Be flexible—change careers.** Growing up, we are given some general guidance for choosing a career: If you love to cook, you should become a chef. If you love to work with numbers, become an accountant. If you love helping people, become a teacher or social worker. If you want to be your own boss, become an entrepreneur. Maybe that's the path you took. But there's no rule that says you have to stay on that career track if it's not making you happy. Discovering that something is not right can be just as empowering as finding what *is* right, suggests Robin A. Sheerer, author of *No More Blue Mondays: Four Keys to Finding Fulfillment at Work*.

Don't let fear stop you from discovering and pursuing your hidden passions. And try not to worry about money. Those who love what they do and have fun doing it tend to make more money than those who don't. You owe it to yourself—not your parents, friends, or spouse—to be content.

"Don't Quit Your Day Job...Yet"

NEW YORK, APRIL 30, 2004

For some, the desire to enjoy both work and life can only be fulfilled by striking out on their own and starting a business. At the 2004 Nia Enterprises Leadership Summit in New York, several successfully self-employed sisters shared how they made the transition from full-time employment to full-time entrepreneurship. Are you ready to make the leap?

Heather Davis: Welcome to our entrepreneurial session. I'm the vice president of sales and marketing for Nia Enterprises. Here to moderate our first entrepreneurial breakout session, "Don't Quit Your Day Job . . . Yet," is writer Hilary Beard. Hilary, along with panelist Lisa Price, co-wrote Lisa's autobiography, *The Sweet Smell of Success,* which was published Ballantine Books. In it they describe the inspiring journey that Lisa took to become the owner of the popular Carol's Daughter line of body-care products. Hilary is also a health writer and former editor for NiaOnline, as well as a freelance journalist with clients such as *Essence*, *Health*, *Odyssey Colour*, and *Pause* magazines. She's currently completing *Venus and Serena: Serving from the Hip*, a two-book series on values for teens and tweens with Venus and Serena Williams.

Hilary's own journey to becoming a full-time writer started in corporate America. Before striking out on her own, she graduated with honors in political science from Princeton University and then advanced through sales, marketing, and general management positions with Proctor & Gamble, Johnson & Johnson, and Pepsi.

Hilary Beard: I'm excited to be able to bring you these outstanding panelists. We have wonderful information to share with you about growing and developing and changing, and we hope that some of you may learn some information that may even change your lives..

Seven years ago I was sitting in a panel, not so different from this, about how to become a writer. I was in a corporate job. At that point in time, I was with Pepsi doing new business development for them. And for years I had been dreaming of transitioning into a life where I would have more autonomy and could be more creative. But I was afraid that I would lose my financial security. I was raised to take a safe job so I could support myself, as many of us were. I was afraid that I would spoil a wonderful-looking resume. I was afraid that because of that—if I left and didn't succeed, I wouldn't be able to go back.

Little did I know that I would never want to go back. But I was afraid and many of you may be experiencing that feeling. When I went to work at Pepsi, I already knew that I wanted to leave and I kind of parked myself there at a level a little bit below the radar screen. And every now and then someone would tap me for a position, and I'd come up with some reason why I couldn't do it. That was only going to last for so long, but I got away with it for as long as I could.

In the meantime, I quietly dropped out of my graduate program in business and I began to take creative writing programs in the evening. Once I started to take creative writing, other aspects of my creativity began to blossom. I started taking dance classes (which I had always wanted to do but had never done before) and I started taking different art classes. The more I [took classes], the more my creativity became alive, and I began to envision possibilities for my life that were not possible when my time and space and energy were kind of controlled by somebody else.

But as I went through that process, it became challenging, because I had these dreams for things and I didn't know how to get to them, and I was in this environment where my time and energy and efforts were constricted every day. So I started experiencing conflict. Part of how I managed myself through that conflict was that I shared with a couple of co-workers, who I was very close with, that I had dreams of doing other things. I found out that they did, too. And we were all parking there under the radar, planning something else.

So rather than only doing business development and strategic plans for Pepsi, the three of us got together and we tapped into some other people. We would meet on a monthly basis and we wrote strategic plans for ourselves. We would meet monthly and we would hold each other accountable for the things that we had identified in our plans. We decided that our lives were more important than the work that we were doing for Pepsi. I was terrified about some of the tasks—I mean, I had to break thing down into the smallest tasks, like, "Call Temple University's—(I live in Philadelphia)—Adult Education Program and order a catalog so you can take an adult-ed program for creative writing." I really had to break it down.

But once I started identifying things that weren't too scary to do, I started to build my confidence and began to take bigger and bigger steps. And then the universe just came at me and opportunities came at me so quickly that a five-year plan turned into a one-year plan because everything moved very quickly. I had no idea that skills from corporate America would translate into a creative life and help me transition more quickly. And so if any of you are creative people, know that they will transfer, and of course they will, if you're business people.

I left Pepsi in 1997 and one of my first opportunities was at NiaOnline as a senior channel producer. So my mortgage was paid, my car note was paid, my gas, my electricity, and my phone bill were covered. That was great. Shortly thereafter, Lisa Price and I were able to land a book deal, and shortly after that the Venus and Serena book deal kind of came along. So things just moved very rapidly, because my skills transferred and people wanted a writer who could get things done on time and honor her commitments and could manage her time.

And so I transitioned into a life that was more wonderful than I ever could have imagined. Shockingly, to me, by the second year of working for myself, I was earning a salary that was equivalent to my corporate salary. So much for starving artist—that fear went right out the window. And now I have a greater and greater vision for what is possible for me, even as a creative person. I love that I'm able to go for four-mile walks in the morning, go to yoga at 10 a.m. if I want to. I feel I can really take care of myself. I believe that this transition has really strengthened me and will extend my life because I've found balance—mentally, physically, and spiritually.

So perhaps some of you today have a side hobby or an interest that you've always been interested in and you've been working on and have a vision for your life that's different from how you're living today. Or perhaps you're tired of your financial future or your self-worth being in somebody else's hands. You may have dreams for being a bigger person or a more expansive person and doing more interesting things than you're able to do right now. If any of those are the case, we have wonderful information to share with you today.

I have three incredible panelists who are going to share information about making the transition from a full-time job into self-employment or entrepreneurship without making a flying leap of faith, with a way to plan it. And if you'd like to make a flying leap of faith, that's wonderful, but there are other ways to do it as well that may feel more comfortable to you.

So they're going to speak with you about how to get your business started while you're working for your present employer; how to get support, either from your current employer or from colleagues in your environment to make the transition; and then, finally, how to plan the transition itself. So, we're looking forward to making a presentation to you about some of these types of ideas. Then we can have a really intimate dialogue and hopefully share information with each other so we can support and nurture each other's dreams moving forward after this workshop.

So with that, I'd like to introduce to you our three

panelists. Immediately to my left is Vonetta Booker-Brown. She is president and founder of a virtual assistance practice, Right Hand Concepts (righthandconcepts.com). She has over eight years of experience in writing, editing, graphic design, and web design. Her client roster is really very impressive: it includes CB Commercial, UBS Warburg, Pitney-Bowes, Southern Connecticut State University, Weekly Reader—remember them?—Essence Communications, Daymon Associates, and PH Factor Productions.

She creates press releases, bios, and media kits for small businesses. And she's creator, designer, and editor of Triscene.com, which is an online magazine for the New York and Connecticut areas. She's an accomplished journalist and writer, and she's contributed to various publications including *Essence Magazine*, Essence.com, *Vibe*, *Honey*, *HealthQuest* (which is a magazine I used to edit), and MediaBistro.com, so we look forward to sharing with Vonetta this morning.

Next to Vonetta is Yvette Moyo, who's here all the way from Chicago. Yvette is president and CEO of Resource Associates International. She has committed her life to the positive promotion of African American talent, tradition, and culture. She's best known for creating two brands, Marketing Opportunities in Business and Entertainment (MOBE) and Real Men Cook for Charity. I'm sure many of you have attended a Real Men Cook event. It's the largest urban, family-oriented Fathers' Day celebration in America and it takes place all around the country. It's a wonderful celebration. I've had the opportunity to attend it in the past.

Over $200 million in business has been generated among firms that have associated with the MOBE enterprise. It's very impressive. In addition, she's an avid internet marketer and manages Mobe.com, RealMenCook.com, and

ZelpahMoyo.com. She's a member of Illinois Congressman Danny Davis's digital task force. She serves on the NAACP Reciprocity Initiative Committee—I'm curious about what that is—and has served as the NAACP ACT-SO [academic competition] judge. She was recently recognized by *Network Journal Magazine* as one of the twenty-five most influential black businesswomen in America.

And then Lisa Price, down at the end, has become a personal friend of mine over the last several years. We embarked on this odyssey together of documenting her story. Lisa is an incredible woman with a passion for fragrances that she did not know could be made into a very successful business enterprise. And over the last ten or so years she has transformed that gift into Carol's Daughter and Carolsdaughter.com. The boutique is located in the Fort Greene section of Brooklyn. She started out of her home in 1993 and opened her retail store in Fort Greene in 1999.

One of the most incredible things, I think, about this woman—because we talk so much and we thought so much about how I had to have my money together before I could make this move and we wanted everything to be in place— the truly incredible thing to me about Lisa, in addition to the wonderful woman that she is, is that she created this business while she was bankrupt. So much for the notion that everything has to be perfect in your world financially for you to create a business. While we were writing the book, I would think, "Okay, twenty-five people work for you, but you're bankrupt, right?"

It took a while to compute that the laws of the Creator supersede the laws of man when you have a purpose. So, I'd like us to begin our conversation. We're going to start with some straight business questions, but at some point in time, I am going to ask them to expound a little bit about their relationships with their creative spirit and what role that played in their development, because I know for all of them it played an important role. So the first question has to do with how to make time to start a business when you're working a day job and at what point do you know—how do you know—when it's time to cut bait and leave the security of your day job and take the step into your own personal venture?

Vonetta Booker-Brown: Well, I think it's a good opportunity to use the time that you're at your full-time job to map out a plan. You can take the time to really research the industry that you want to go into. That is really the main part of it. You really have to research, find out about the business that you're going into, figure out if it's going to be profitable. Who are your competitors? What kind of products are they offering? And perhaps you can find a niche in which you can offer something that they don't have.

Also, of course, when you're in a full-time job, then you're still getting your steady paycheck. So you can really use that to save up for your rainy-day fund. Just basically use that time to prepare in different areas.

But for me it was really an experience because I worked as an administrative assistant and so I had a background in that, as well as on the creative side. I worked as a freelance writer and editor and I've also done web design as well as graphic design. So, for me it was a period where I had to kind of look into myself because I wasn't really satisfied with the position I was in. I was doing administrative stuff, but I knew I could do much more than that, based on the skills that I'd acquired over the years. There really wasn't room for growth there.

As far as the virtual assistance industry, that's something that I looked into and I thought, "Wow, I can do this." Basically, I provide administrative assistance and creative support to businesses and individuals via email, phone, and fax. And it's really growing just because of the internet and everything. Once I did research on that, it just clicked. Like Oprah says, it's like an "ah-ha moment." I was like, "AHH!" I said, "Wow, I can really do this." I mean, as far as moving to another position or working for somebody else, I really couldn't find a position that utilized all of my interests and all of my skills.

And as far as virtual assistance, this is something that I could tie with everything that I can do: administrative, web design, copyrighting, press releases, all the things that I have done; I could combine this under one umbrella and go into business for myself, which is something I always planned on doing.

So it really just clicked. It was kind of like a spiritual light bulb that clicked on, like, "this is something that you were meant to do." So I always felt that I have the backing of my faith and everything. It was just something that told me that I needed to go ahead and pursue this. And God was like "Look, I'll have your back, don't worry about it, just prepare and plan."

Yvette Moyo: I absolutely agree that while you're working for someone else, it's a great time for self-examination. Self-examination, know thyself. What are you made of? What makes you tick? Everyone is not cut out to be an entrepreneur. And you really need to know, not fool yourself to think that you just want to be president. There's so much more than that, because that means: can you wash the dishes and sweep the floor and empty other people's garbage? Can you clean your bathroom and your office if you have to when you start out?

You have to really know how low you can go, because it's a rollercoaster and I always say—well, this year has been my most difficult year in fifteen years—I always say, I knew it would be a rollercoaster, I just didn't know how low it could go. And in those dark moments I knew myself, I knew that it's not about what I see but it's what I know about myself.

During the opening session [of this summit], I think someone was talking about going for the jobs that are the "stretch jobs." And you want to do that because if you don't like the stretch, if you don't like being on a stretcher like this all the time, or for parts of time, then it's just not good for you. I wouldn't recommend entrepreneurship if you don't like making decisions, or hurting people's feelings— and I'm really not good at hurting people's feelings. But I found a way to do it. Because you have to hire, you have to fire, you have to be the one that makes the decisions.

And you watch that other employer, watch those people at the top and see if you can do the things that they must do as leaders. Everybody is not a leader and it's not anything to be ashamed about. I was sort of like the super volunteer from Girl Scouts, Brownie Scouts, all the way up. I was a super volunteer. So I felt that that spirit in me would say that I could do anything for my job, if I could do anything for anybody else. Everybody doesn't have that kind of spirit.

Some people are like, "Pay me! Pay me today!" And you need some of that, too. You need a lot of that in business. But I think you want to go looking for things that entrepreneurs have to have. You have to have sales appeal. I had an eleven-year sales career. From age twenty-three to thirty-four I was in sales. Heather Davis and I were side by side in our sales positions—she was at *Essence* and I was at another magazine—and selling is difficult.

You have to hear "no" over and over again. So I would say, keep the day job but also get a position—not in the grocery story or in a jewelry department where people come and they know what they're going to buy, but go somewhere where people aren't really sure that they're going to buy something and you have to convince them of the value and find things that you believe in. But do that in the evening. And I recommend highly that you go ahead and work somewhere that is sort of entrepreneurial. There're a lot of other things that you can do where you can sell things and get some experience organizing, closing deals, keeping track of money. You can go back and do better, set new goals as you understand how things work, and reach higher and higher.

Do some of that at night because, as a business owner, you will be working like you have two jobs. And I do this constantly and people say, "How do you keep yourself sane?" Well, at some point I said, "What did black women do [in the past]?" I mean, I'm hurting, but what about in the Depression, what about in the 1930s, what did people do? Well, they held together. They shared what they had and made it through and they worked two jobs. They worked doing people's dirty laundry. I mean, can you really think about that?

Sometimes I think about what it must be like to have to do somebody else's laundry. I take care of my ninety-six-year-old grandmother, I do her laundry. But can you imagine somebody you don't even know, taking their dirty laundry? I think back about the women that had to do that and say if they could do that then I can do this. I can go have my dinner and I can visit with my husband, I can say, "See ya, I have to work from nine-thirty until three-thirty to get a project done." Then I work until three-thirty in the morning and still go to bed happy. That's what it takes. But keep your day job until you see if that's what you're made of. That's my recommendation.

Lisa Price: If you happen to have a job and you don't like your boss or a co-worker and you keep saying to yourself, "When I have my own company, I'm not going to have to do this, I'm not going to have to put up with him or her," well, you're wrong. You will, times twelve. So, I think the best thing to do, if you're in that type of situation, is to pray for the person that you work with that you can't stand and try to learn how to better deal with him or her. If you stay in that negative place, "I hate my job, I hate my boss, I hate the woman who sits next to me, I hate the manager in the art department," you're negative and what positive is going to come to you? What ideas are you going to get? What creativity is going to flow? You're going to be blocked.

You have to try to find a way to love them. Send them light and just ask for patience within yourself. It will come in handy so many times over, because when you have your own company, you will hate employees, and then you have to pay them. And I'm not saying that to say that everybody who works for me is awful. That's not the case at all. But there are times when [for them] it's their job, while for you, it's your baby. It's your heart, your life, the blood that flows through your veins. For them it's just a job. So if they get ticked off, and you're not too far away and you hear them call you the *b*-word, it's like whoa, wait a minute. How much did you earn this year? When did you want that day off? You know?

So having that kind of understanding and compassion for people's flaws, for their mood swings, is very important. Then you also gain a certain respect for those same bosses that you can't stand because once you become a business owner, you recognize all the crap that they had to deal with that you didn't realize when you were their assistant or their right arm. When you need someone who you have to depend on the way your boss used to depend on you, and you can't find that employee—you can't find anybody with that dedication—then you say, "Oh, my God, Mr. So-and-so, how did he handle the twelve of us back then?" It's a great place to start because it gives you an opportunity to put your feet into somebody else's shoes and see if you can still walk.

It's very important to know that you can live without a paycheck, because even when you get it, you have to put it back into your business. You're never so fortunate to say, "Oh, all of this is mine," because there's always a new software thing, a leaky roof, somebody else that has to be hired, a consultant that you need for something and you constantly have to be able to give back. I was fortunate that the universe placed me into a career that trained me for being an entrepreneur. But I didn't know that that's what I was going to be.

I used to work in television and film production. So I got used to working without a paycheck. When I was bankrupt, I could not get credit cards, so I couldn't incur debt. So I had to learn to live within my means, learn to live on a secured credit card where I gave them money and they held it for me and I charged and paid and charged and paid. During the time I worked in television and film I had certain expenses. I had rent, I had cable—I have to watch TV, I'm sorry, it's my weakness. I had gas, I had electricity. But my life was structured so I knew, when I was earning money in a television or film job, I would save or try to pay off my debt, because I had a tax bill that I had to pay as well. And when I was on unemployment, I knew that I could live off of what I was earning.

Television and film is very unpredictable—you work two days, you work a week, you work a year. Your show gets canceled, you come to work on Monday and find you have no job. So, that atmosphere taught me that if I don't have a check every week I can handle it. That's really important because you have to pay your people first, you have to give back to your business first, and you get paid last. So if you think about that, as you're thinking about whether or not you can do this, it's a good thing to plan for.

Listen to yourself and really, really examine what it is that you want to do. You might think right now that you want to start a web company if you're good at computers, even if you don't really like computers. You imagine you can do it since you do it at work all day for twelve or fourteen hours, so you think you can do it for yourself. Not if you don't really like it. You will give up because you will hate it. Right now you do it because you're going to get that paycheck, and you have the health insurance and the company car or whatever it is that you get. When you have to do it for yourself at two o'clock in the morning, after working on a project with your child for school and you're doing the laundry at the same time and you're exhausted, you have to love that thing that you do to stay up at two o'clock in the morning and work until six and then get the kids up and get them out to school and start all over again.

So know that you love the thing that you're going to do because you will have to get up in the middle of the night to do it. I heard that on an *Oprah* show and I realized that I was in the right business. I can't tell you how many times it came true—that I had to get up in the middle of the night and make some cream. And I still do. With twenty-five employees I still get up in the middle of the night and make some cream.

So, love what you do and get comfortable with that boss mentality and that atmosphere and embrace those people that you can't stand. See yourself hugging them. You will learn so much from them. I can't tell you how much you will learn from them when you put yourself in their shoes and look at the world from where they're standing.

Vonetta Booker-Brown: I just want to touch quickly on something. Both of you made great points. I'm interested in what you just said about praying for your co-workers. Because we all have at least one co-worker like that. What worked for me is that I let them kind of propel me to do my thing. I had this one co-worker who sat next to me, all she would do is just complain, complain, complain. She hated her job. She'd say, "Oh God, I can't . . ." all the time. And I would say, "Okay, well, why are you still here?" And she would say, "Oh, I'm too old." She would have an excuse as to why she couldn't. So I let that fuel me. I did not want to become like her.

I always believe that if you're not satisfied with your situation, then you ask yourself, "What can I do to change this?" And I was dissatisfied with where I was and so I was kind of like, "Okay, well, you know what? I really need to stack my chips and prepare and do what I need to do so that when the time comes, I'll be ready to step out on my own." Because I did not want to end up like her—really bitter towards everyone else and just negative.

Hilary Beard: Okay, great... We also want to talk about the transition process. At what point do you begin to share your plans [to start a business] with your manager or co-workers? And is it possible, particularly in today's competitive environment to do it in a way where you can enlist their support?

Yvette Moyo: I'm not the best person to answer that question because I sort of just stepped out on faith. I was very much in love with my husband and one day, while we were dating, and I was going from city to city with a sales position that took me all over the country, he said, "You know, if you weren't married to that job, I would marry you." And I was sort of like running downstairs, and I turned around and said, "What?"

He said, "You're married to the job." And I'm like, "No, I'm not." He said, "Yes, you are." So then I said, "But then repeat what you just said, because I can quit the job." He said, "No, you can't." I said, "Yes, I can quit the job." And he said, "What would you do?" I said, "Anything." "You know, I don't believe you," he responded. And that's when I really began to plan [to go out on my own]. But I didn't have the supportive situation. You know whom you work for after eleven years. I knew my boss would say, "I'll put a contract on you if you leave here." I was in sales and bringing in all the money.

I could not share what I was going to do, but one of the things that I had done was to maintain my credit rating. This is really an important point, just from a practical point of view. I was spending everything I was making because I was really living the great glamorous life. And at thirty-three years old, I thought I was the bomb. I was making good money. And I wasn't really saving a lot of money, but I did have a great credit rating.

While you are working for someone else, make sure

that you're working on getting that credit rating. I don't think it's the amount of money you have, because I've seen people just go through tons of money to try to prove to other people that they can make their business work. And I'm one of them. But it's the credit rating that will give you leverage and will give you respect when you walk in the door with an idea. But you still have to have a track record and by working that night job, or something, you can show them a track record on the entrepreneurial side, which gives you some points. But the credit rating is everything.

We spend much too much of our money on dumb stuff. You know we look good in anything we wear. Nobody cares if you wear the same thing twice to church in a month. When I was working I thought, "Oh, my God, I have to rotate this stuff. I probably can't wear this stuff the whole season to the same church. Maybe I ought to go to another church."

But it doesn't matter. It does not matter. It's just how you line up spiritually. And it's also what people can look at in black and white, because there's no other way they can judge you. You'll stand there and say, "But I'm a good person. You know, I don't want to go bankrupt. I don't want to give up the business." And they'll say, "You don't have anything here [on the balance sheet]."

Right now the last two years have been incredibly difficult. I market the positive things about black people, about our culture. That's what my business is really all about, bottom line. But this is not a market for that. And then, on top of that, we have Real Men Cook, which is really a way to make sure the world knows that we do have black men who do responsible things. And they cook because they're raising money for charity; that's what Real Men Cook is all about. Nobody cares about that. And so we lost an incredible amount of money and we shoved our money into our dream.

...All of our creditors were calling, saying, "You know, I'm looking back and—what happened?" They'd ask me, "What happened?" And I would be able to tell the story. I had a client for a quarter of a million dollars for three years, and one day he called and said, "I'm not going to be back." And then another one for four hundred thousand, another one for fifty thousand. It was devastating, excruciating.

But they looked back and saw that we paid our bills on time, that we were honest. Some people said, "You should just file for bankruptcy." I said, "But I do business with people who look just like me. That means they wouldn't get paid." They would not get paid, and that's what kept me going. How can I represent black people and just say, "Forget you and too bad, I'm going out of business and I'm going to start a new business tomorrow"? That's the American way, to leave people hanging.

So I just want to say that while you're working on your job, find out what your credit rating is, and try to get a higher credit rating and establish a track record. That really is like your resume when you start your own business.

Lisa Price: I was in a situation in which I could share what I was doing with the people I was working with. I think it's easier when you are not a threat to them, and also when they see that you do the job that you're supposed to do. I worked for a cable startup network. And they had fancy computers and fancy software and things that I'd never had in an office before and definitely didn't have in my home. At that time only rich people had computers in their homes because they cost two thousand dollars back then. There were no $599 computer models from Dell.

I wanted to be able to design my labels and brochures on this fancy equipment. So I let them know that I have this company, making body-care products. I will purchase my own paper and toner, but I'd like to be able to use the equipment after hours, if it's okay, to work on my projects. I was working with advertisers so I ended up getting all of this free, fantastic advice because they said, "Well, let me read your brochure." And "What do you make? Bring some stuff in. Here are some marketing ideas and here's this tip and here's that tip." So many things they told me were wonderful. I couldn't afford any of them because I didn't have any kind of budget at that time. But they were all very supportive.

It started with me coming into the environment, doing my job, coming to work on time. They knew they could depend on me, they knew that I wasn't going to not answer their calls, and that I'd take care of my stuff. And when I needed to work on my things, I was there at eight o'clock in the morning or seven o'clock in the morning until seven o'clock at night. And there was trust. They knew they could trust me, and they knew exactly what I was doing. So there was no subterfuge. It's very hard when you're trying to be sneaky and hiding and you look shady and they don't know what you're doing. Is she stealing paper? What's going on?

So if the opportunity presents itself, I think it's very important to share what you're doing and you may get good advice. But if you know that you're going to go into the same field, or you know that your boss is petty and catty and you can't share, then don't. And work on it outside of the workplace. Work on it on your own and, if the door opens up and you can go in and try to get some advice from someone, then do it. But you'll know your situation better than any of us will.

Yvette Moyo: It's funny that you mention that. I wish I had an experience like yours, but unfortunately, I couldn't do that with the employer I was working for at the time. I'd seen them operate with some co-workers. If you told them you were doing your thing, they would get frightened and reacted with this attitude that was like, "Okay, maybe we should kind of get her out."

When I was at work, I did the work there and I was able to manage my stuff on my own time. Which gets to the point that you brought up before about balancing the two. I think that's really important to see how you can operate as an entrepreneur. You have to wear many hats and you have to be very disciplined. So I was working this full-time job and doing my thing on my own time. When I told my employers that I was going to step out on my own, I said, "Here's what I'm planning to do," and that was basically when I gave them my notice. It was a little longer than the standard two weeks. I think it was three weeks or a month. I basically said, "Okay, you know, this is how I'll set things up for whomever you're planning on hiring in the future."

Hilary Beard: Good, I'm thinking that we might have just answered a little bit of the next question in the process of answering this. I shared with everybody what my planning process was. I actually had a plan. And not only did I have, in effect, a business plan for myself, I knew that I was deficient spiritually because I felt like I was lacking in courage.

To the point you were making, Yvette, I felt like I'd come from all these courageous people and here I was. I had everything but I was chicken. I just really felt dissatisfied with myself around that. So, in addition to a business plan about making the transition, I put together for myself a spiritual plan to learn more courage. And week by week by week I gave myself assignments to stretch myself spiritually so that I would learn that if I put myself out there, if my intentions were good, if I used my gifts and talents, then the universe would respond and I would get all these signs. And time just collapsed and a five-year plan just—boom! All of a sudden I was there.

So if that resonates, it might be worth trying. I put in place for myself a spiritual support system. I started spending less time with my friends from work who all wanted to do other things but were very fearful. I had that tape in my own head—I needed to stop hearing it—the "You won't succeed, you won't make enough money, you'll be homeless. Oh, my goodness. I could go from living in a beautiful home to homeless in like thirty seconds." So I knew I had to work on that about myself.

Vonetta Booker-Brown: You've got to keep it positive—I think that is the most important part. It's the mindset. I really feel that you just have to surround yourself with positive people because you will have those people—and they may be co-workers, they may be your family members—who, if you tell them about your plans, they'll kind of like look at you and say, "Why do you want to go out on your own? I mean, hello! Steady paycheck, benefits. Why do you want to leave all that?"

Some people just don't get the entrepreneurial mindset. That's just a fact. So I feel it's really important to surround yourself with family and friends who are supportive, who really believe in what you're doing. You want to have that encouragement. You want to surround yourself with people who are going to support you. That's one of the aspects of this.

Yvette Moyo: So much of what I talk about every day is just about God—about how good God is, and tapping into my spiritual self and just repositioning myself spiritually. I felt like I lost so much: I destroyed my credit rating in two years. Then I got a letter from a banker who used to be my great friend, but when you get a letter from your banker that says nothing's working, you really have nothing.

But why do I see stuff? I know that I'm on a whole other plane. My husband, who also quit his job, had eight school-age children when we married. And I had one. So we had nine children. I am God's child. I know myself and my co-workers. When I was dating him, I thought, "Well, you know, you don't ever want to get married to him, 'cause, God, look at his past." But I think he's great. I'm his fourth wife. We've been married fifteen years. We've done excellent, great things together. I'm his *last* wife.

I know it's a wonderful story and I won't go into it but it is stepping out on faith, knowing yourself. When your friends tell you, "Girl, you better get rid of him," you don't. Because you know that it is a good, positive thing and you know that it is something. For me the spirituality is everything. And for those of you who haven't really tapped into yours, this is a great workbook: *How to be a Powerfully Positive Person.* And I saw a girlfriend of mine who wrote this and I said, "I read about your book on a website. I'm on a little budget but I brought my little twenty dollars today to get your book." I bought the book and she said, "I just love you. You're so positive."

I'm in the book. She acknowledges me in the first paragraph after her family and with George Fraser and Les Brown and people like that, she has me in here. I was shocked. I got cold on the airplane when I read it. But you guys need to get this. It's got all kinds of action plans. It's by Joel Martin and it's titled *How to Be a Powerfully Positive Person*. You'll find you can make yourself into a powerfully positive person. I've never seen anybody say it as beautifully as Joel—that they went on a faith journey to sort of bolster their faith, because it's about your spiritual journey. Everything in life is a spiritual journey. You cannot separate your spirit from what you're going to put your name on. If you do, that's why businesses fail.

One day I was in a workshop and somebody said, "Why do black businesses fail?" And so everybody raised their hands to say, "Poor service"—you know, the usual black stories. And the moderator said, "No, because they give up too soon."

So the question is really: how long can you hang in there? You must understand and know that things are going to work out. It may not be in business. I just want to make sure nobody goes out of here to just start a business. It's extremely hard. It is really hard. I mean, it's excruciatingly painful to watch things that you believe in seem to go up in smoke. And you can then see that you're the only one who sees that that's really a beautiful thing, that smoke.

Lisa Price: I can't really tell you how I planned it because I didn't really plan it, the universe planned it for me. And I had to listen. I'm a workaholic and when I worked in television and film I learned how to work even more and even harder. So I was always thinking, "Well, I have to get out of debt, I have to pay my bills, I have to improve my credit rating." So I probably would have done the day job and the entrepreneurial job for even longer, but I became pregnant with my first child and I realized, well, I had a baby to take care of, I had a job, and I had a business. When would I ever see my child? And how much money was I going to have to pay a babysitter to keep juggling that schedule?

So I didn't get to plan when I was going to leave and when I was going to quit. It was just like, "Look, it just doesn't make any sense, you've got to quit." So I stopped working a month before my son was born. And it was a good thing that I did that because things kind of took off from there. So the universe knew what was going on and I just wasn't listening. I was being stubborn.

Hilary Beard: Okay, why don't we open it up for questions? You've heard some outstanding information and I'm sure it spurred some questions. Anything anybody would like to ask?

Summit Delegate: I've always known that I want to start my own business. But I'm married and I have kids and the biggest struggle that I've had has been, "Okay, I've got to take care of the kids. I've got to have health insurance." So I know a couple of you have kids. How do you get past that? That's like a huge roadblock for me in terms of the fact that they've got to have insurance and they've got to eat. If it were just me, not a problem, but how do you do it when you have kids?

Yvette Moyo: For me, it's creativity. And the kids have got to understand that what you're doing is important to them. They become your best cheerleaders because they want to say, "My mommy owns her own business. My mommy does this." And you incorporate them from the very beginning in the business so that they don't feel like you're taking anything away from them. You know, value added is what we all look for and what you have to do is make that business, starting the business, "value added" for everybody involved.

Go to the Small Business Administration and other women's networking programs and find out about group insurance plans that you can get into. Start planning now, as you're keeping that credit rating up, so you're also planning and putting money away to cover your insurance. Maybe for the first year you'll pay it in a lump sum. Maybe with the first client you pay that in a lump sum.

Take care of that because you can't afford to get ill and you have to take care of your children. But let them know that there are going to be a few things they're going to sacrifice, because you're going to start the business. Then find out about free, fun things that kids can do. I know about a lot of them. Believe me. We have led the good life on a small salary but it's about creativity. One thing that business ownership will do is free you up to look for those kinds of things.

Lisa Price: You may have to work and not necessarily spend as much time with them as you want. You're going to have those moments when you can't be there. But you have so many more when you can make it to the poetry reading at ten o'clock in the morning or the puppet show or the carousel ride—the things that other mommies can't come to because they have to answer to someone else's schedule. So it does give you more flexibility and you have to explain to them, "Well, Mommy has to work now but remember when we did so and so? We're going to do this activity on Saturday."

Summit Delegate: You [Lisa Price] mentioned that you were bankrupt. Was this when you were trying to start your business? And if so, how did you get creditors to loan you money? Or was it a matter of going to private investors to start your business?

Lisa Price: The business paid for itself. I just kept investing in it. So I had to do things slowly and I had to do things in a comfortable manner, selling out of my home because I couldn't afford rent on a store, so I was manufacturing the products in my home, living in a fishbowl, with ten employees in my house and customers in my house and that kind of thing.

We did everything by prepaying for our materials. I would budget what I needed and how much I would have to pay for the materials, and then how much I would make and how long it would take me to sell it, and then how much I would get back and then what I was going to reinvest. We didn't have an American Express corporate card until 1997, 1998, and that was actually obtained by my husband because his credit rating was better than mine. So he was the guarantor for that so that the company could have that card. But still you have to pay it in thirty days. But that was my first taste of having a minute to wait before I had to pay for something.

I didn't have a bank loan until 2001, and at that point my bankruptcy had passed and I had paid my tax debt. And I used that loan to help renovate the warehouse so that I could finally move the business out of my house. So it was slow and I was constantly reinvesting in the business. If I could go back and do it over again, I wouldn't do it differently be-cause of what I learned, but I wouldn't say that everybody has to do it this way because it is extremely difficult, but it was the only way I could do it.

Summit Delegate: I want to share a little bit before I ask my question. I'm actually an entrepreneur, and I own my own business, which I incorporated in 2001, and I just left my corporate job in January 2004.

Hilary Beard: What do you do?

Summit Delegate: I have a clothing company. I'm a designer of two lines, a bridge collection and a contemporary collection. And I guess what I really want to share with you is that my corporate career was in the field. I had a field job so I was kind of disconnected from the corporate environment, which really enabled me to do a lot of things independently and kind of on company time. My cell phone would ring, and who would know really who it was? So there was really no perfect circumstance but I think being in the field really aided me to be able to start it and keep my day job for as long as I did.

What propelled me in January to leave my corporate career was that my company started outgrowing my ability to give it part-time attention. The one challenge, I guess, that I have right now (considering it's only been about three to five months) is that I've been the doer at all times. But I'm really, right now, in a kind of a growing pain. So I guess my question to the panel is that once you've started, and you have a machine that's going and going, how do you transition from being a single entity, doing everything? When do you make that transition to start bringing people on board? Not that it's a financial barrier but when is it time? What are the signs that it's truly time? I'm still working twelve- and eighteen-hour days.

Yvette Moyo: I would say you should start hiring when you see that you're dropping balls, when you start to be late and you don't remember things, because you always want to be perceived as doing what you promised and doing it on time. I don't know if it's an age thing, but sometimes I don't remember. You've got to call somebody up and say, "What did I say?" When you start doing that, you really need a backup person. And I would say that you could start with a part-time person because it's very expensive to pay the government and the taxes and all that. And if people want insurance, and you can't afford it, you can start by hiring somebody part-time, or hiring an intern. For example, you could find a more seasoned intern who's worked out in the world before and plans to go back to get their degree and might just want to work a couple hours a day. Or maybe somebody just had a baby and doesn't want to go back to an eight-hour-a-day job. But when you start feeling like you don't have a handle on this, you really need to bring somebody in. That's just what I'd say.

Lisa Price: Your job is creative—you design a clothing line. So when you start to not create anything for a while, you can't come up with an idea, something doesn't feel fresh, it's probably because you're too bogged down in other details that someone else can do. You cut too many patterns, you pinned up too much fabric, you went shopping for ribbon for hours—things that someone else could do for you. So then your creativity starts to suffer and your business suffers. So you have to remember to put you and your business first and when you feel that one or the other is suffering, it's time to get help.

Vonetta Booker-Brown: I actually have two daughters and it is a big jump when you relinquish that salary and relinquish that health insurance and there's that complete transition. But let it not be a fear issue. There is no perfect timing. It all just kind of gels and works.

Hilary Beard: Coming back to the health insurance tips, you can join an association, there are unions you can join, and there are different plans available online. I know, for myself, it was good to start investigating that while I was still employed, because it was a big unknown. Oh, my God, you can't leave, you have benefits. But then once I understood that I could purchase them, I was like, "Okay, I can afford that." That demystified it and made it not quite so scary.

Yvette Moyo: One of the things is that business goes up and down. There are good seasons and there are not-so-good seasons. And the opportunity to reinvent yourself or diversify is something that you have to keep in mind. And one of the things that we did when the economy wasn't really good for things that were specializing in black people—which is right now—was to come up with a product line, because we have great brand recognition with Real Men Cook. These events are held in ten cities on Fathers' Day. But it's more than the event, it's the spirit of the event. We're promoting positive family activity.

So we came up with a Betty Crocker cake mix that's under the Real Men Cook brand name. We have about six other products that'll be out. This first product is Real Men Cook Sweet Potato Pound Cake. So that's just an example of how you've got to keep your creative juices flowing. You've always got to think about recurring revenue, which is one of the things that we didn't have in the event business when we were doing big things that cost half a million dollars to produce through sponsorship. And when that sponsorship base falls out, where's your recurring revenue going to come from? So the idea was how do you get the equity out of that brand? We knew we had brand equity. And so this is it. Now the consumer can do something.

Hilary Beard: I wanted to share a thought that inspires me and may inspire some of you. One of the things I learned about myself working in a corporate environment was that I began to look at the source of my income, the source of my well-being, the source of my happiness in life as being something outside of myself, as being this corporation or these businesses that paid me and allowed me to have a certain lifestyle or way that I moved in the world.

Part of what I've learned out through the process of stepping out on my own, is I've reconnected with the spirit of who we are from. We are from the most incredible people in the history of humankind. I mean, social Darwinism, survival of the fittest, we are it. Ain't nobody been through what we've been through, and we're still here to talk about it. The people in this room have had the benefit of an incredible education that people from around the world get in shipping containers, get in little boats, find all sorts of ways to try to get it. These people try to get access to the kinds of things that we have and take for granted, and may have lost touch with about ourselves.

The women in this room, at this conference, in this country, we're incredibly educated. We're in companies that do just incredible things and have technology. We have incredible skills but sometimes if you're pounding your head into that concrete ceiling or if you're not getting the promotion that you believe that you deserve, sometimes you may start to question yourself or just lose touch with what you have.

I know Yvette said something that I wrote down: "It's not about what I see, it's about what I know." And so many times it comes from your imagination. It comes from the creative bringing things to you. All of these dynamics come into play once you make yourself available and say, "Yes, I want to do these things." Amazing things will happen to you beyond what you could ever imagine or plan. So I wanted to share that thought.

Summit Delegate: Yes, I want to share one thing. I'm still working. I still have entrepreneurial pursuits. One of the things that I find really important is not being afraid to talk to people who are doing what you're doing. And also to take classes. That's a great way to learn more about what it is you want to do. From a floral design class that I took, I realized that I had an incredible gift. And coming home one night from that class where we made some wonderful arrangements, a woman said to me, "Where did you get that? I've got to have that. I'm having this activity and I need twenty-five of those." I was standing in the middle of New York, because I was trying to get to Penn Station. I didn't want to be afraid, but I didn't know whether I could replicate this splendid thing I'd made. So I wanted to just say, we shouldn't be afraid. We shouldn't be afraid to take classes and learn things about what it is we think we'd like to do.

It's also important to ask questions to people who are doing what you'd like to do, to be able to learn more from them. Out of my own passion, I started to talk with other women who are doing this flower thing. And one very, very, powerful, fabulous woman said, "Well, why don't you come down to the shop and make a few arrangements and do a few things?" And then, my passion for it began to grow, my expertise in the area began to grow and then people started coming to me saying, "Can you create something for me for a special event?" There are houses that I decorate for the holidays.

If we have all these talents, we shouldn't be afraid to explore them. But mostly, don't be afraid to ask other people because I think we sometimes feel it's very competitive: "If I tell her I'm trying to do this, it's going to negatively impact my building the business." But I think that that kind of energy just propels us. Look at other people who are doing what you're trying to do as a beacon and not as competition.

Vonetta Booker-Brown: That's a big aspect of research. While you're doing your business and you're still working at your full-time job, don't be afraid to pick the brains of the people in the business that you want to go into. I have never really encountered somebody who just said, "No, I don't want to help you."

Because there's something flattering when someone comes up and says, "Hey, you know, you're really doing your thing, can you talk to me about how I can...?" Most people understand that and they welcome that. At one point or another, most of us, or most of the people that you encounter, have had to do that. I mean, everybody had to start somewhere.

Lisa Price: Also don't be afraid to fail. It's okay. It happens. You make mistakes, you fall, and then you get back up. And when you get back up, you're stronger because you can look back on what made you fall or what contributed to it and you can help yourself. So don't look at it as if you have to be perfect and everything has to be right and you can never make a mistake, because you're human and it's going to happen. But it's okay. It's what happens in business. It's what happens in life.

Hilary Beard: And sometimes things that look like failures really aren't. In the short term it may feel like a failure, but a month from now, or six months or a year, you can see the larger pattern that it played into and that something greater was being formed by releasing something.

Yvette Moyo: That reminds me of one thing. Don't put a period where God has put a comma.

Group: [Laughter]

Summit Delegate: I say that every day!

Hilary Beard: Okay, good. Thank you very, very much, panel.

12

MORE ADVICE FOR

Transitioning
to Your Own Business

Many sisters are boosting their incomes by starting sideline ventures. They enjoy the combination of having a steady, full-time job and running their own business part-time. And why not? A full-time gig serves as a financial anchor to support yourself, your household, and your business prior to generating profit.

There may come a time, however, when you decide you are ready to leave the world of nine-to-five altogether and devote your attention to this business. To do this, you need to evaluate your own readiness. Part of that preparation means having three key elements: (1) a sufficient client base, (2) enough money stashed away to live on while your business launches, and (3) the necessary resources to run your business at least for a year. It takes a lot of hours, sweat, and patience to run a successful business.

Do you want to know, once and for all, whether you have

what it takes to make the transition from part-time to full-time business owner? You should take these steps before making the leap:

Learn how to write a business plan. You need to know your business inside and out, as well as your customer base. The best way to achieve this is by writing a business plan. A business plan will help you build on your company's strengths and work around potential weaknesses. It should include a description of the business and key players, market and customer research, sales and distribution information, and financial calculations. There are various resources that can help you write business plans, including classes offered through local small-business organizations. Also check out the Small Business Administration's online tutorial, as well as books and software available from Bizplans.com. Realize that your business plan is not a static document and should be updated yearly. Also keep in mind that you will need to show a business plan if you intend to secure money from a bank or venture capitalist.

Get your finances in order. You don't want to be so stressed out paying bills that you won't be able to concentrate on your business. Pay off as many debts as you can. At the same time, start setting aside money in a separate money-market account that's earmarked for your business. The amount you save should be based on the funds you need to live comfortably (to cover rent, groceries, utilities, and so on) and to run your business (including business supplies, personnel, and taxes). You will also find it easier to get a business line of credit down the road if you already have equity of your own to back it up.

Put together a group of informal business advisers. Today's smart businesswoman looks to business alliances. A business advisory board can have a few as four or five people who help the entrepreneur run the business and solve problems as they arise. Corporations have a board of directors, which helps develop policies and has some fiscal responsibility. Directors are usually given ownership (shares of stock) in return for their participation. An advisory board, however, is an informal group that doesn't assume financial and legal responsibility for your company. Typically, these folks volunteer their services. Tap into personal contacts and mentors to find possible members of your board. Also look to such organizations as the Service Corps of Retired Executives (SCORE), your local Small Business Administration, local businesswomen's groups, purchasing councils, and professional or trade groups. Join the local African American chamber of commerce, which will enable you to network with potential clients and other professionals in the business.

Engage your family in your plans. You will certainly need the emotional support and cooperation of your family, particularly your children and significant other. Make sure you discuss how your full-time business interests and pursuits may affect them. Tell them about the downsides (struggle and personal sacrifices) and the upsides (success and prosperity) of this venture.

Make time to affirm and take care of yourself. Remember that you are the most important asset of your fledgling business. It is important that your schedule allow time for rest, relaxation, and exercise. The more physically and mentally fit you are, the easier it will be for you to overcome any obstacles and deal with the pressures of running a new business.

PART 4

BUILDING YOUR DREAM, INC.

13

In Pursuit *of* Purpose

Sometimes it takes more than one wake-up call before you realize that it's time to run your life, rather than allowing it to run you. Here, Cheryl Mayberry McKissack—who is Nia Enterprises' founder, president, and CEO, and one of this book's editors—shares her personal story about how she finally "got it" and started the company of her dreams.

Eight years ago, I found myself at a crossroads with my professional objectives and my personal needs. I had allowed my life's purpose to be replaced by a goal of financial independence. As the vice president of sales for the Americas at U.S. Robotics, a global information technology company, I was succeeding at that goal: I *was* financially independent. Furthermore, I had recently married my long-time love.

Though I was happily married, there was still an emptiness inside of me that I was unable to fill or shake off. I realized that instead of experiencing "joy," I was simply going through the mechanics of life. I asked myself: How did this happen? When did I lose my joy?

Life is too short to spend without joy—this had become clear to me a couple of years prior. A reminder of my mortality had been delivered in the form of a large tumor that developed suddenly on one arm. After being rushed into surgery to remove it, I found out that the tumor was benign. Still, the experience was an epiphany for me, about how life can change dramatically in a matter of moments! I vowed then to make some changes in my life. Two years later, at the crossroads in my life, I reflected on whether I had been true to my words and made those changes.

I had not. In fact, my life had become a series of meetings and deadlines, with the focus on winning the next big deal! U.S. Robotics was my life and my first priority. It was not unusual for me to call my husband, Eric, on a Friday at midnight and tell him I was still at the office and was unsure when I would arrive home.

Furthermore, when Eric invited me to his work-related events, I would frequently arrive right in the middle of the program, with all of his colleagues and their spouses already in attendance. I did my best to look as if I had been leisurely preparing myself all afternoon to attend each event, when in truth I usually rushed in from my office in the suburbs through rush-hour traffic to make it on time. I knew I was in trouble when my husband, one of the kindest and most supportive men in the world, politely told me one day that he would appreciate if I would just wait and arrive toward the end of an upcoming company event for clients.

I was embarrassing him. At the time, I justified my actions with the fact I really did intend to arrive on time! My justification came from the pressures of my career, which were deflecting my responsibility to change focus. There were numerous warning signs that I needed to take control and create some balance in my life; however, it would take a series of major events and several more years before I would decide to make any significant changes.

The first transformation happened when U.S. Robotics, which I had treated like a spouse, was unexpectedly sold to 3Com at the height of its success. I was headed for a divorce! Though surprised by the decision of the CEO to sell, I decided that, perhaps, it was for the best. Now I could take a much-needed mental and physical break to try to reclaim myself and focus on my new marriage. I made plans to take off a year from work to experience all of the things that I had put aside in recent years. I also underwent major surgery that I had been postponing—putting my career before my health—because of the recovery time involved.

However, within five months of leaving U.S. Robotics, I accepted a new position at Open Port Technology. Once again, I was addicted to the corporate drug of meetings, deadlines, and trying to hit the big win one more time! Never mind that I just had major surgery and had not finished healing—I was ready to go one more round. During my next two years at this software technology company, I went full-throttle as the worldwide senior vice president and general manager. My days became a blur of activities, such as increasing our revenue, developing our marketing and product management operations, expanding our European operations, launching our Asian office in Hong Kong, and raising venture-capital funding for our company (not to mention collecting thousands of stock options that would eventually be worthless, suitable only as wallpaper for my home).

One day while on a business trip in Italy, I realized that something was very, very wrong. Despite all my many blessings, I had never felt so empty in my life. I no longer felt a rush from creating a new product or celebrating a big win. In fact, I had a difficult time simply going to the office and maintaining focus throughout the day. While I knew that I did not want to continue what I was doing at the time, a vision of my next step was escaping me. How could I recapture some of the joy that I had previously felt?

I started with an old tool that I had updated for my purposes, called the "Ben Franklin" grid. It is based on a journaling exercise that Franklin devised to chart a path toward "moral perfection." First you start with a blank sheet of paper. Then you draw a line down the middle and list your perceived strengths and weaknesses in opposite columns. Next, on a separate sheet of paper, you list several goals you would like to attain in your future or current job. Finally, you assess those goals with respect to the strengths and weaknesses you listed in the first sheet, with the aim of determining which goals will maximize your strengths, minimize your weaknesses, and bring you the most joy. For instance, what if one of your stated goals is to advance in the sales field, but one of your listed weaknesses is that you're afraid to fly? Instead of taking a sales job that requires a lot of air travel, you may decide that you're better off taking one with a local territory.

In my case, I divided my goals into three categories: professional, personal, and civic interests. In the professional area, the most important goal for me was the development of an opportunity that would involve my passion for information technology. My background in that area was a strength.

In the personal area, the main goal was that my next venture would allow me the flexibility to spend time with my family and friends. As mentioned, one of my weaknesses was not focusing enough on my personal life. I also wanted that venture to give me the flexibility to pursue a variety of outside interests, such as teaching, corporate board affiliations, and writing. With respect to civic interests, I wanted to see how I could include "community" in my day job. I knew I had the energy and desire to make that happen. I needed to create an opportunity that would allow me to make a difference and give back some of the blessings that I had received.

With these insights, I focused on molding these goals into a professional opportunity. One of the tools that I learned early in my business career is how to define a problem and then use creativity to solve it. My basic objective was to take my primary professional interests—technology and data—and try to come up with a suitable business concept that would also allow me time flexibility, variety, and civic involvement.

Meanwhile, I had recently read several articles talking about shifting U.S. demographics and the rise of minorities as a larger percentage of the population. I decided to explore that angle further. I started talking with colleagues who were involved with making decisions at corporations that serve this changing demographic. My research included looking at how data was being handled for the African American market. While some companies had exceptional methods of procuring this information, I found that the majority of these were going about this in an ad hoc manner, with little discipline in their approach. The idea continued to expand after I uncovered what I believed was a breakthrough opportunity.

The opportunity was to provide a solution for gathering data about the emerging African American market, and give corporations better information for providing this growing market of consumers with products and services. My premise was further reinforced by the fact that African Americans were and still are the largest consumer group, in terms of buying power, among all U.S. minorities. This led me to develop the idea of connecting and accessing African American women and their families through the internet. That took care of my information technology goal. I was further able to integrate my goal for community and "giving back" through the offerings that would be available, including health information, business and lifestyle content, participation in leadership summits, scholarships, and community leadership recognition.

The final step in completing my plan was to develop a name that would also symbolize the attributes that I had identified as important. That task would prove to be a bit harder. I initially selected the name *Brown Angels*; however, it did not meet the approval of several of our NiaOnline writers. We went back to the drawing board to develop a name that went with the concept. After much discussion of the name, the word *nia* was brought up. Nia means "purpose" in Swahili, and it is one of the seven Kwanzaa principles. The crowning glory of the name is expressed in our logo, created by a wonderful design firm based in Chicago, Art on the Loose. The "Nia head" symbolizes the spirit and strength of the African American woman, additionally displaying a sense of knowledge and purpose.

People ask me all the time why I decided to focus on this specific market. I tell them that I wanted to come from a position of strength, focusing on an area where I had a strong sense of comfort and familiarity—where I could add some value. In 2001, I had the opportunity to present our fledgling company in front of venture capitalists at the Springboard Enterprises Venture Forum for women-owned businesses in Chicago. As

I told the audience, in response to a question about our ethnic focus, "It may come as a surprise to you that I have been an African American woman all my life and my experiences are my secret weapon toward my understanding of this market."

Today, Nia Enterprises LLC provides an online community, called NiaOnline (www.niaonline.com), and delivers research and marketing services focused on African American women and their families. Our goal is to provide purposeful information that will have an impact on the lives of our families and communities, and in return to encourage our members to voice their opinions and provide feedback on their buying habits and preferences.

We have been blessed by many experiences throughout this journey, and I can truly say that I have been given the opportunity to live out my purpose every day. I believe we are all responsible for creating our own world of joy. My personal world of joy includes the experiences and professional challenges of running my own company. While I have no personal desire to return to corporate America, I love some of the challenges and opportunities that exist in today's corporate business environment. I have an opportunity to satisfy this need by serving on both corporate and civic boards. I am constantly presented with new challenges and growth opportunities, such as co-editing *The Nia Guide* series of empowerment books, and I have recently been presented an opportunity to teach a class at my alma mater, Northwestern's Kellogg School of Management. Last but not least, I continue to be rewarded by time with my family and extended family. Life is indeed good, and I am so grateful for these many blessings.

I remember having read Russell Simmons's autobiography, *Life and Def*, several years ago. In his book, Russell offers a quote that summed up the focus of his future as compared to his past. He offers this perspective:

Life is about finding happiness. It is that simple. As I said, the only real happiness is the kind that comes from within, and I believe that my happiness only comes from serving other people. When I started this book three years ago, I was uncomfortable about writing a memoir while I was still so young. Now, I realize the timing is perfect, because while my first forty years were about consumption and money and power, I am hopeful that the years to come will be about service.

Simmons's perspective defines for me the basic "purpose" of my future. My goal in my life is to incorporate giving more. I believe that through this focus I will continue to discover and live my true "purpose." This purpose continues to be the fundamental principle for my future and this season of my life.

"Finance
Your **Dreams**"

NEW YORK, APRIL 30, 2004

Let's be honest: a balanced and fulfilling life often requires funding. During the 2004 Nia Enterprises Leadership Summit in New York, several financing experts and entrepreneurs discussed strategies for financing your dreams.

Laura Washington, Moderator: In this session we're going to touch on what lenders and investors want to see in your business plan. But that's just one aspect of it. The main focus will be on strategies for financing your dream once you actually have a business plan in place. We have five panelists with us today.

First we have Reta J. Lewis, who serves as vice president and counselor to the president of the United States Chamber of Commerce, the world's largest business federation. Reta has more than twenty-five years of experience as a government affairs and public policy professional. In her capacity as vice president and counselor, Lewis is one of the chamber's experts on issues affecting small business and is also charged with leading the chamber's strategic initiatives designed to build alliances and partnerships across the United States. Reta previously served as special assistant to U.S. President William Jefferson Clinton in the Office of Political Affairs.

We also have Cheryl Mayberry McKissack, the founder, president, and CEO of Nia Enterprises, a Chicago-based database, systems-integration, and marketing-services firm founded in January 2000. Nia Enterprises provides opt-in, permission-based, marketing-data solutions related to the growing and specialized market of African American women and their families. McKissack has received several recognitions, including the top twenty-five Chicago Women in Technology award and being one of the twenty-five companies selected to present at the 2001 Springboard Venture Forum.

We have Shirley Moulton, cofounder and president of Universal Solutions, Inc. (USI), a full-service, national, information-technology consulting company. USI has been supporting the IT needs of diverse businesses since 1983. Shirley began her career with Atlantic Richfield Corporation in Philadelphia in 1977 as a staff auditor in the area of corporate finance and accounting. In 1979, she joined Sun Oil Company in Philadelphia where she was a senior financial analyst in the corporate finance division. After leaving Sun Oil, Shirley collaborated with members of her family in 1983 to establish USI.

Please also welcome Janice Cook Roberts. Janice is executive vice president of the New York City Investment Fund.

Roberts joined the Fund when it was launched in September 1996. The Fund provides financial and strategic assistance to businesses that spur economic growth in New York City. Chaired by Henry R. Kravis, the Fund has raised over $95 million in capital, and its investors include many of the city's global business and financial leaders. Prior to joining the Fund, Janice helped oversee foreign video operations at Universal Studios.

And last but not least we have Laura Washington. Laura is associate editor of *Consumer Reports Money Adviser*, a monthly newsletter that provides a trusted resource for personal finance planning and everyday insights to protect and grow consumers' assets. Laura began her career on the staff of *SmartMoney*, then moved to *Money*, and was a *Redbook* magazine columnist for several years. She has covered everything from investing in the stock market to tax breaks for victims of 9/11 to insurance and retirement issues for a variety of publications, including *Essence*, *Fortune Small Business*, the *New York Post*, *Self*, [and NiaOnline]. Laura has appeared as a finance expert on numerous television programs and stations, including CNNfn, Lifetime TV, and "Good Day New York."

Let's start with Reta. What are some chamber initiatives that every woman in this audience needs to tap into now?

Reta Lewis: It's interesting. I talked to Laura and Cheryl about participating today, and I will tell you that it really does my heart good to be in a room where you can look at and see people that look like us. Cheryl and I met at an Office Depot conference, and there were a thousand women at that conference. And I think it was probably about a ninety-to-ten ratio [with regard to ethnicity], and we were probably in the ten.

But one of the things that I was brought to the Office

Depot conference to talk about was women breaking out of their comfort zone. People in the United States Chamber of Commerce always start off by asking if there any women, or people in the room that are members of, or participate in any state, local, regional, or national chamber of commerce? [Show of hands among delegates] So we have a couple.

And the reason I do that is that it goes straight to the indication of where we are, and how we network. The chamber is the largest business federation in the world, and it brings together medium, small, and large businesses. I'm a counsel to the president at the chamber. And when most people think about us, they think it's the Department of Commerce, but we're not government funded. It is a private-sector, non-profit, over $130 million organization. The United States Chamber of Commerce is the national umbrella, I would call it, for the state and local and regional chambers, of which we have about three thousand members.

From places around the country, many chambers of commerce would probably belong to the national chamber and look to us for advocacy issues on national and international issues.

And we are also composed of over 850 national industry associations, and that could range from anything—or any idea, I like to call it—from the National Carpet Association, all the way up to radio and TV associations, recording studios, technology associations, anything of that nature.

We have over 100,000 direct members. So we represent a universe of about three million members. And I like to explain it that way because that is a very, very powerful network. And it is a network that I've been constantly saying to women, saying to people of color, saying to minorities, that we need to be in—whether it's national, whether it's state, whether it's local.

Why? That's where all the deals are being made. Anything major that is going on in your community—any company that is coming into your community, any major project, ranging anywhere from infrastructure to where they're relocating different facilities in a community. Any of your regional chambers of commerce are probably not only involved in that, but are probably leading the effort in that community, and they are working very closely with their state- and local-elected officials.

I love to participate in any type of session where you are working and networking with women. I always tell people that it is always very comforting. We know it. We know each other, or we have a natural affinity. But I find it a little difficult when we are asked to go and to participate at a table where it is about advocacy and it's about policy, and it is not about civil rights or social rights or human rights. It is strictly about the business. And so when Laura asked this question, I come at it from that vantage point, and I look at three different areas of things that chambers of commerce, as well as the United States Chamber of Commerce, really have to offer individuals who are either thinking about starting a business, are currently in a business, or are talking about how they're going to grow and expand their business.

Because I think there is a niche market there, or niche place for each and every one of you. And the chamber works because such entities are about one thing and one thing only, and that is being the premier advocacy organization nationally, as well as state-wide and locally.

And when I say advocacy, I mean that if you take any issue that matters to business owners, whether they're male or female, whether they're black, they're white, Hispanic, you name it, we are all concerned about the same issues. We're concerned about healthcare. We're concerned about new technology. We're concerned about whether we are going to get one of the largest infrastructure bills that is going to go on in this country, that's going to buy jobs. We're all concerned about how we market ourselves and gain access to the international marketplace.

But it is in those discussions that you're not only going to advocate, but you're also going to participate with other players in the room who are going to talk about the issues that affect your community, on state, national, and local levels. And so I'm always advocating for women and minorities to participate in those types of efforts.

And on much more of a practical standpoint, the chamber in 2003 launched a small business tool [http://www.uschamber.com/sb/default] that just has thousands and thousands and thousands of pages on it, that, as a chamber member, you can go visit to get access to everything about growing and expanding your business.

And one of the key areas on there is about finding out how to begin to participate in finding the funds that you need to grow and sustain your business. It's an online tool that we have that serves a practical need, even more so for small businesses, more so for businesses led by people who are new to the business arena. And it's a place that offers not only financial information, but pages and pages of different resources.

We also work very closely with all of the different government agencies in Washington. So, for any area that you're probably thinking about looking at in terms of either continuing to grow your business or start a business, we offer links on the U.S. Chamber's website that you can then click on, to be able to go in and learn about agencies, especially if you're looking at and thinking about things like government contracting.

Laura Washington: Thank you. So you definitely need to get in there for networking, to learn about issues that are of concern to all businesses, and to find out about government contracts and that type of thing. You've all either reviewed or written business plans. I'd like to ask, what is the most crucial element of the business plan when you're looking for funding?

Janice Cook-Roberts: When people talk about real estate, they always say location, location, location is so important. And I guess when I look at business plans, I really feel that the management team is critical to any business plan. You really have to have strong, experienced management. Either you've worked in an industry—you know how it works, you have a unique idea that's going to serve a large market—or you don't know the area, you haven't worked in the industry, but you are certain about your idea; then I would say to partner with someone who does.

Because for someone to come into my office and say, "I want to start an HMO for Medicaid recipients," oh great. But if they don't understand the HMO market, which is highly regulated and incredibly complicated, it's going to be hard for me to have confidence that they're going to be able to launch a business like that. Because every business faces challenges somewhere down the road, and you really have to feel comfortable that the management team has the ability to make the turns and overcome those obstacles, because they're going to be in those businesses every day. I'm going to give them money and I'm going to be there to provide some assistance, but I'm not physically there, so I really have to trust that that management team knows how to grow a business.

I think the other important aspect is that there is a large market, and that they're going to be able to dominate and get a nice share of that market. That's the other important aspect.

And then three, for me: are they going to be able to pay me back in five years, as opposed to twenty-five? We look at that very seriously, so we look at projections, and are they reasonable? If I reduce those projections, am I going to get paid back? Because the number of times that I've seen a business actually hit their projections is rare, because stuff happens. So it's very important.

And it's also important to understand what kind of business you're going to have, and what type of capital you should seek. Should it be debt? Should it be equity? There are lots of different ways to finance a business.

Laura Washington: Thank you. Shirley?

Shirley Moulton: I had those exact two points. I think that crucial to any business plan is a team and their capabilities and their passion. One other thing is how you react when you're faced with obstacles, because any business has cycles and ups and the downs. And it is in those down moments when you have to really dig deep and see what you're made of. So I'm not sure how you identify that sort of stick-to-it-iveness, I guess that's the word, and passion, that this business is in your DNA and that you're going to stay there no matter what. Because a lot of times when the numbers don't add up, it is that stick-to-it-iveness that gets you over.

So I am with Janice on that. It is the team and their passion, and also that large target market, and also a sustainable model, something that's going to sustain, and you sort of can reinvent yourself as you go along. So that's what I see.

Janice Cook-Roberts: Also, when I look at a team and I want to see that they are passionate, that they are going to stick with it when the business is really tough—one way we measure that is how much money are they putting in? And it doesn't have to be a half a million if they're raising two million. But it has to be significant enough that I know they have worked hard for this money. It could be fifty thousand dollars. This is their life savings, their net worth. The Small Business Administration, if you're going to get a loan from them, often requires collateral—that you sign over your house. They require this because they want to know you've got skin in the game, and you are not going to just walk away from this and say, "Sorry, I tried, it didn't work, I've got to move on."

So that is one way I measure it. I think it's important if you're starting a business to give it a lot of forethought, so that you start putting away money. And it doesn't have to be a huge amount, it just has to be enough to show a bank or a fund that you are serious, and you're willing to put your money in there too, at risk.

Cheryl Mayberry McKissack: I want to look at this from maybe a little different perspective, as an entrepreneur, since I think you really have addressed all of the things regarding financing of business that have been told to me. What they're telling you is exactly what people who are thinking about lending you money are going to have a conversation with you about. And you've got to be able to answer those questions.

The way I would look at it is what can a business plan be for you? How can you use it as a tool? I've written a lot of business plans and I've read probably more than I care to. And I will tell you that one of the things about a business plan is that it really should be a working document. Most people write business plans, and they go and they try to get funding and they never look at them again. I'll tell you, it's very interesting to go back and look at your business plan, and see where you are.

Janice mentioned how she's probably seen very few businesses where the projections are actually met within the time frame. And that's because most entrepreneurs are very passionate about what they do. And so you're going to tell the best story possible. And there are all of those things—9/11, the economy changing, the stock market crashing, the highest jobless rate in history—those things you don't think about, because basically, you don't have control of them, but by the way, they do control you.

And so the business plan can be a great working tool. And for some of you that I know here who are thinking about starting your own businesses, I think the other thing that it will allow you to do is to really sit down and see whether or not you have a real business. You might have an idea, but an idea is not necessarily a business. It will help you by putting it on paper and answering some of the questions.

And you can get a very simple, very low-cost business planning tool. There are many programs that are out there. They don't cost a lot of money. And they'll kind of walk you through the kinds of the basic things you need to include in your plan. And if you can't really answer those questions, or you're not sure how you would do it, you need to answer those and make sure you're comfortable with your answers and that you have some contingencies before you start your business. Because if you start your business and then start to deal with all those things, it's probably going to be too late.

So I would look at it just from the standpoint of how you can use it as a tool. And by the way, you're going to write it and rewrite it, and probably rewrite it again. And if you're doing that, you probably are growing and doing something. If you've written it once and haven't looked at it for three or four years, it's probably not of any value to you.

Reta Lewis: I'd like to ask a question. How many that are currently here have their own business? I always find that a fascinating question, because you're either in a business or you're thinking about starting a business.

I will tell you—and we hear this all the time—that access to capital is the number-one issue facing any business, whether it's starting, whether it's growing, whether it's expanding—especially if it's for women, and especially if it's for minorities.

Over the last several years, I've definitely seen different methods that women can use, and tools that they can go to, in order to help them if they're beginning to look at starting a business.

A lot of people ask the question, "If I'm thinking about starting a business, where are some of the places that I can go?" I will tell you that whether you like it or not, whether you think it's great or not, the Small Business Administration, nationwide as well as within your region, and within your state and local area, is really a good place to go for resources, and primarily it's because they run what they call women business development centers.

And in those women business development centers they

also have small business development centers. It's people there who are really able to give you the technical assistance that you're going to need. Yes, there are programs, and we all can go online and we can find a tool, but nothing beats going into a place and sitting down with someone and having them help you and work you through your great idea, moving it to a great plan.

One of the things that we do know about women and minorities who are starting their business is that most people start their businesses by using their credit card. Credit cards and family and friends—that is a proven fact. You can hear that data time and time and time again. So before you can even get to the stage of looking at it from any other angle, you have to look at the relationships you create. If a venture fund is looking at a million dollars, a lot of people will think, "Well, let me go to my bank. Do I have to get my banker?" Well, of course you do. We all know that's about one thing: it's about relationships.

But even before you go to your bank, or your family or your friends, you have to have a business plan. If I'm going to loan someone money, or give someone money, or invest in their idea, or invest in their company, I want to know: Do they have a very, very strong business plan that I can see? What are they going to do with my money? Can they pay me back?

And now I think that people are really being a lot more stringent because family and friends are asking those hard questions. My brother has his own marketing business, and he came to my parents and said, "I want to expand my business." And my father, who is in business, said to him, "Send me your business plan. I love you a lot, and I know you're going to pay me back, but I need to see your business plan. I need to know what you're going to do with that money."

Because, you know, he's asking him to go to the bank and get a loan on his behalf, because he couldn't go to the bank in New York City to get the hundred thousand dollars he wanted to use as an infusion to grow his business. So my parents said, "We love you, but I'm seventy-two and I'm seventy-six, and we're at the retirement stage, and I'm not going to put my house up, and my business up, and my trusts up, in order to—you know, I love you, but I do need you to sit down and talk me through what your vision is."

I think what I can see from a practical standpoint, from the whole family and friends strategy, it really is about your passion. It really is about the passion that you have a great idea, and it's something you know you do, something you know you do well, and something that you have researched significantly.

And I think one of the things that I've definitely seen is that it really is about the data and the research. You need the data and the research to show that there really is a market out there for that product or that service, or idea that you are trying to put forth, that you want to have people give you money for.

And it's no different when you sit down with the women at the Business Development Center. They run classes. It's really basic. They will run classes that you can go to and sit down and participate in with other women like yourself who are trying to do these things, whether you're starting or growing or expanding. So there are a lot of peer networks that you can get into that are really, really basic, separate from the fact of always looking for mentors of women in this room who have their own businesses, who can tell you about the start to finish as you are moving your idea to fruition.

Shirley Moulton: Can I just add something to that? Something very, very different from this conversation. A lot of times when you get into a situation, in these kind of theoretical situations, none of this stuff works. It's not practical.

Let me tell you about our business. It's twenty-one years old. We started with zero business plans. I never owned a business plan, never did a business plan. My brother-in-law was reading *Venture* magazine and we decided that the computer age was coming. And in 1983, Microsoft was not even a public company—please appreciate. And we started out in 1983 on absolutely nothing but a shoestring and a passion, and an idea that says—which is similar to yours— that there was a market, there was a large market. It was coming. It was the second coming of Christ, and we knew it and we didn't care, and we had no business plan.

And quite frankly, we weren't able to get a million-dollar line of credit, so we started with the social capital, which is friends and family and credit cards. So you move from that into maybe your financials and your numbers, kind of show- ing a little bit of credit-worthiness, so your small, local bank will loan you ten thousand dollars or fifty thousand dollars.

And then you move from that into having stron- ger numbers, to support a million-dollar credit line. We didn't have a business plan. We started a business plan when we were forced to kind of rethink our strategy maybe back in 1990 when the market got very competitive. So we had to put that down on paper, like, "How are you going to survive? And let's put a business plan in place to sort of guide us there."

As Cheryl said, it's so interesting. It really is a living, breathing document. And you kind of stay with it, even though sometimes you forget, you really have to. And sometimes now I'm so excited that there are online tools where that business plan can almost pop up with your email notification—go read this page on such and such a day. But it is a living, breathing document, and it is when we sort of got in trouble that we did, in fact, come up with a business plan. So I just want to share that side.

Janice Cook-Roberts: But I think that is important, too. Friends and family are kind of the starting point, if you're doing a startup business you don't have a lot of experience in, because those people know you, and they can tell if you really have a passion. If you come into my office and it's the first day I meet you, and you're not saying, "I'm putting my house on the line," I have no way to know what your passion is. It's very hard to determine that, whereas your friends and family know you, it's character lending, which there isn't as much of. I think there used to be that, when my parents came along. They don't do that as much anymore.

And so if someone were to come to me and say, "I have this great idea, I know it's going to work," I would say, "Okay, great, go get a customer." So you have to go get that money from friends and family that's going to give you a little bit so that you can incorporate and set up your business, and so you can go and have a conversation with someone who might say, "Okay, great. I'm going to give you a contract."

And then when you come back to me and say, "I'm starting, I've got a contract, like you said," I may then say, "Okay, I'm going to give you a little money. And then when you get that second and third and fourth contract, I'll give you a little more." But I think that's where friends and family really can come in and help get you started.

Laura Washington: So Shirley, you started out with your own money, with your family's money. But by the time you went to institutions to get funding, to get the million-dollar line of credit, by that time you had a track record.

Shirley Moulton: Absolutely. You have to have that. And anybody, if they talk about how access to capital is so difficult, remember that it's not difficult if you have the numbers. It's only difficult when you don't have the numbers.

Janice Cook-Roberts: On this side [laughing]. Last night I was out until nine o'clock at night because I'm looking for deals. I'm looking. Every time I meet with my board, they say, "We want you to be more aggressive about getting this money out so that we can have a bigger impact on the city." So it's a two-way street, I guess.

Laura Washington: Okay, credit cards, friends, family, your house, savings. So that's the seed money. You get the seed money from your friends, your family, your credit card, yourself. Sometimes you have to be innovative when it comes to finding money, because you keep going back to the well. As an entrepreneur, you're not going once. You're finding the seed money and then you have to go back when you need to expand and grow the business. Statistics show that African American women are less likely to tap into institutional lenders than other business owners. So I'm wondering, what are some other resources out there for funding that people don't think about?

Cheryl Mayberry McKissack: Let me start with that. One of the reasons we put this panel together is that we wanted to bring you kind of a representation of women who were involved in a variety of different financing options. Because I think one of the really important things is that you try to be as creative as possible.

We talk about friends and family, but in this particular day and time, a lot of our friends and family aren't going to give us any money, either. So that is not necessarily as much of an option as everyone talks about. And credit cards and debt and all those kinds of things have some of the same issues.

Certainly, for what Janice is talking about, which is certainly more of a venture capital model, and money from funds, you do have to be able to prove yourself in this day and age. The day when people would take a lot of chances as a startup are really somewhat gone, at least from my perspective. You have to have a track record. You have to have revenues. You have to have clients. You have to have all the basics you have in a business.

So one of the things that you may want to consider when you talk about friends and family—and I think Janice talked about this a little bit—is why do friends and family give you money? They give you money primarily because they love you, because they believe in you, and they hopefully have had an opportunity to see you be successful in some phase of your life.

Now, it could be one of the above, it could be to just get you out of the way so you won't ask them anymore, or it could be all of those things. But typically, it's because they've had a chance to see you be successful in some part of their life. They believe in you, and they're willing to put their money in and invest in you.

For those of you who have jobs today, and who are not yet entrepreneurs, consider that perhaps your business idea can help an already established company achieve a particular product, or particular service that they're interested in.

You may want to think about starting your business by out-sourcing and providing that service to a company.

And it's not necessarily going to give you the millions and millions of dollars, even though it can, and I'll tell you about a situation where it did. But it will allow you to get started, and typically, that money is not debt. So basically, you are providing a service, you're getting your business started, you're able to reference a particular major client, and with that, hopefully, you will be able to get others. And so that's another way to look at financing your business. But obviously, you've got to have a skill, and you've got to be doing something that somebody is interested in sponsoring.

One of the things that helped us start Nia was institutional money. We did start Nia with our own money, and believe me, we had to provide that information upfront. But also, the way that we survived was not through that money, because that was not really the bulk of our money. The way we survived was that we had a Fortune 100 client, and we were fortunate enough to get that Fortune 100 client to sign a three-year contract with us, the day that we started our business. And the reason we were able to do that is because I had a co-partner at the time who had worked for that company, and they knew her—they knew what kind of work she could do, they knew the qualities that she had, and they decided to bank on us.

They weren't going to bank on it just because they happened to like her. We also found at that particular point in time that they were interested in finding a vendor to help them with the work they were doing,

So the combination of timing, the combination of relationships, the combination of the credibility, the combination of all those things, faith and God and prayer, and having the right person in that corporation at the time and every-thing else that went on—*that* made the decision.

Now, I will tell you, probably six months after the deci-sion was made and we got our first check, the person that made the decision, who was a very high-ranking person, was let go of by the company. The company went through a major reorganization. Since then, every person in that com-pany that helped make that decision is no longer there. We were high five-ing all the way down the corridor, and then, six months later, we were kind of like, "God, I hope the new people know our name." So it's not a definite, but we man-aged to keep the contract through the three years, and that really was what allowed us to survive. It's just an optional way that you may think about it. And by the way, it's not debt. They own no equity in our company.

Shirley Moulton: I was just thinking about what Cheryl was talk-ing about. And another idea too, if you start a products busi-ness, you can actually start out small and go out and be very vigilant about getting credit, even though you may not have any credit, and magically you get a credit line from some of your vendors. And the other side to that—on the service side—is also trying to get the retainer up front if you're in a service business.

Janice Cook-Roberts: And then as far as once you're in business—if you have customers, and you have accounts receivable where you've sold something, you know someone owes you money, and it's a good customer—there are places where you can go finance those receivables, so that you can continue to grow your business, and you don't have to wait for that money to come in, because oftentimes your customers may pay you after thirty days, sixty days, ninety days. Schools, for example, will pay you, but it just may take forever.

And so in the meantime—if they're lenders, it's called factoring—they say this is a good receivable, I'm going to buy it from you, and you don't get a hundred percent of that money, but you'll get 80 percent or 85 percent, so that will allow you to have cash so you can continue to grow.

Shirley Moulton: Just to piggyback on that, you have to watch your margins in those situations. If you're a product company and you have tight margins, factoring is very tricky, because it's almost like loan sharking to me. So you have to be very careful.

If you're in a service business though, when you have more play with the margin, you could probably take a chance on doing that. In most cases, you'd be surprised. A friend of mine has an imaging business in Michigan, and right before they went bankrupt, Kmart gave my friend's business an advance on a contract of seven hundred thousand dollars, cash. They had not even started. Cash on the line, before they started one ounce of the work. So look for those kinds of deals. Don't be afraid to ask.

Janice Cook-Roberts: That's where women are different from men. Women are so proud, and so thoughtful, and, think, "I'm going to do this, I'm going to plan it out and I'm going to do it," and then you get a plan and you're just like, "Well, I'm just going to stick to my plan." Don't be afraid to ask and take a risk, because all they can say is no, and you move on. You've just got to stick with it.

I've told companies no, and as you said, the business plan evolves. And then they come back to me in a year and

I've said, "You've made good traction, this is great, yes, here's a million dollars." So don't be afraid to go back to people who told you no, once you've made some progress, because if people have money, they want to put it out. It's just about feeling comfortable that they're going to get that money back.

Reta Lewis: I think another thing that is definitely happening in the marketplace that we can sometimes overlook is the whole issue of outsourcing. And a lot of times people think if you think outsourcing, you're talking about taking a job or taking the product, the service or whatever, and shipping it overseas. But right now, in the U.S., companies are looking for people who are in current situations where you have either managerial skills or technical skills, you've created a project or you're engineering that place or whatever. Companies are often looking for opportunities where they can take that division or take that particular service and move it outside of the company.

And if you're sitting there as an executive in that company or as a staff person in that company, you might see an opportunity. People have come to me and said, "I was sitting at X corporation and I knew that they were getting ready to do that, that was going to be the plan. And I said I'm going to take my early out." I've got a lot of friends, especially on the telecommunications side, they're taking the "early outs" from these big companies like the Verizons and SBC Communications of the world, and they're saying, "I want to start a business, I've always wanted to start a business. I've got the expertise, I've got the relationships inside of the company. I'm going to take my 401(k) money that I'm getting from my early out and I'm going to look at how could

I get some additional investments. I'm going to go after it. I'm going to bid for that particular business." And because maybe they either run the business or they have significant control over it or their friends are there, they are able to go and put forth a strategy with their business plan to be able to acquire that business.

So we can't overlook that there are opportunities outside the model of just a basic little startup. Thinking from that level, we can really think about how you can find opportunities in the positions that you currently have, or even with your friends, because people are always looking for partners. People are looking for ways to put together the right type of team to come together to move forward on a project. And they're looking for your skills.

And so one of the things that I always say to women entrepreneurs is to make sure you understand what your skill sets are. Make sure you understand what value you have, not only for your own business, but if you want to go into partnership with someone, or even if you already have a partnership with someone. What is the value that you're bringing to that partnership as the two of you, or a number of you, are joining together to combine to develop a venture?

Laura Washington: Downsizing has its upsides.

Janice Cook-Roberts: The other thing to keep in mind when you're starting your business is to stay very focused. I was just talking to a company and they had a software package for improving reading among elementary school kids, and they were going to distribute it through Barnes & Noble. And then as I talked to them, I understood that they were also going to develop the product, the content. And I thought, there are two different businesses here. This is a lot, and for that development of content, you can get someone else to do it. You can say, "I'm going to pay you fifty dollars to develop this content." You take on no risk, but if they go over-budget or whatever, you don't have to hire those employees, you just buy the content and then maybe later, when you have lots of sales and lots of products, then you think about expanding into other areas so you can be more vertically integrated.

But you can think about outsourcing parts of your businesses. You don't have to do everything yourself. And you don't have to take on all those costs of employees if you're only going to need them for one project.

Laura Washington: So there are a lot of creative ideas out there. Cheryl, you mentioned co-partnering, and that leads me to the last question before I open it up to the audience. They say no one is an island, and that's especially true if you're an entrepreneur. A board of advisors is important for any business. Cheryl and Shirley, and anyone else who wants to address it, how do you identify and recruit a good board of advisors? And at what point do you need that in your business's growth?

Shirley Moulton: When we started out, we did not have a formal advisory board. Later on we did, as we got into that trouble that I had talked about, in looking for expansion and new thinking. We sort of looked at where we were and sort of tried to fill out some of the gaps we had in our company. I come from a finance background and my sister came from a strictly operational background, so we had a gap in the sales and marketing.

So when we went to look for advisory board members, we were looking for people with sales and marketing skills, and we also did not only look to Fortune 500–type entities, because sometimes when you pick people from those companies, they don't understand the entrepreneurial spirit and the frontline activity, and when you can't meet payroll on Monday, they don't know what to do.

We wanted to also have the combination of small businesses and Fortune 100–type people so that as we're growing we can address the Fortune 100–type situation. But we wanted to have "both/and," not "either/or," on our board. And we selected them from our network, actually, just going to conferences, meeting people, getting references. And at the back of my mind, too, my selection was all about a contract. And we were able to get some sizable contracts from our advisory board members.

Cheryl Mayberry McKissack: I don't know how many conferences I go to a year. And I go to conferences that are not just African American women, and that's how I met Reta, at the Office Depot Success Strategies Conference. So first and foremost, I would say, is to really use these opportunities. One of the reasons that we have kept this particular one here in New York very small and very intimate is so that people can walk out of here knowing someone.

If you don't know someone that you didn't know when you walked in here, then I think you really haven't gotten your money's worth, because you should get to know someone here and think about whether that person can be a mentor for you in some way. And mentoring is not just about a whole lot of time, it could be a simple email, it could be a phone call, it could be a reference, a contact.

As far as advisory boards, at what point should you look at that? I think it's different for every organization, but I don't think you have to have a big advisory board to get the value. I think you can start with just one or two people.

And I agree totally with what Shirley says, that you ought to look for people who can augment and strengthen what it is that you don't already have. If I'm really good at sales or marketing or finance or technology, I probably don't need to get people that have the same skills. I want to find people that either have different skills or different contacts. And the contact piece is really, really key.

I sit on a couple of public boards and I sit on a number of nonprofit boards, and any of you who are involved in any kind of board work know that today when you sit on boards, they want you to be providing some kind of value. Well, it's the same kind of thing when you're bringing your advisory board together, or your group of advisors. It doesn't have to necessarily be an advisory board, but think about what kind of value they can provide.

And also, I'll be honest with you, everybody here, including yourselves, is extremely busy. You ought to think about what kind of value you can provide, because I really believe that long-term, for a relationship to work, it's got to be a two-way street. So you may be sitting there thinking, "What in the world could I provide to a Shirley Moulton who's been in business twenty-one years and is wildly successful?" But I bet you there's something that you might be able to provide to her. You may be surprised about that. It may be a contact. It may be an area that she's thinking about. But you've got to size up what kind of value you've got to bring to the table, too. Because over the long term, people aren't just going to keep giving and giving and giving, unless they feel like they're getting something back, and it's not money I'm talking about.

Summit Delegate: Regarding financing, if family is not an option—friends and all those things that you spoke about earlier—are there any grants that would allow us to kind of get our feet on the ground before we approach creditors? Before we say, "I've got this business that I've done so well in and I'm coming to you for more money"? Something that can help out until we get a better background? Something that would help us kind of just get started if those other options were not there?

Janice Cook-Roberts: The hard part with grants is most foundations are supporting nonprofits. And so it's very hard—because we've looked at this—to get philanthropic support to back for-profit businesses. Because one, IRS guidelines make it very difficult, just in terms of charitable giving. They have it in their mind that it's supposed to be a non-profit that's not going to repay you, or something like that. So that's hard. You might start with local micro-lending organizations. I'm sure every city has something similar, as far as organizations that can provide you a little bit of capital to get started. Within the minority community, even though we've come a long way, and we now have folks who've made a lot of money—investment bankers and all that—it can still be a challenge to find capital. Someone told me they still hold onto that money tightly, because it's not like they have three generations where they feel like they've got a nest egg. They're still building that nest. So it's still hard to get money from friends and family. So you're right. So you have to be creative. I don't know if the SBA has anything.

Reta Lewis: SBA does have things. There's what they call 7-J money, and even though that was cut back a little, there is a loan program in the SBA—that's another option for you to take a look at.

The other thing that I think, what we've all said, is even though we're talking about the whole capital question, the conversation I've seen over the last year has really evolved into the whole access to the market, and the market being that corporate market or that government marketplace. And so people who also are either growing or expanding their businesses, or really beginning to look at how will they access more of the corporate clientele—how do they really access the government market? And a lot of people that I have dealt with over the last couple of years, a lot of them are the same way. They have been in government and they see an idea that's getting ready to be outsourced and they start a business and they go after that. So that's another option for creativity.

So I think what we're seeing is that the sky is the limit. If we can kind of open ourselves up, we may see some different opportunities there for us to move forward in a business that's not just started at your kitchen table, but something that really is very substantial. And I think you have to figure out where the niche is that you need to get into to find that work. But in your own states and localities, you can look to the government to at least provide you with some technical assistance and some resources to help you begin your business, and grow and expand your business.

Cheryl Mayberry McKissack: Let me just add one other idea that you might think about. Check some of the local universities. I forgot to mention that. Depending on what your idea is and your skills are, that's where you'll find some grants, and it's a partnership typically, so you might be one of four or five other people. They're looking for certain skills in each one of you, and you come together and they give you a grant to perform this project.

And what that will do, obviously, is give you some credibility and, obviously, if the project's successful, you'll have an opportunity to see what else is available from there, but that's another area that you might look at.

14

Turn Your Passion
Into **Profits**

As a teen, Rachel Duverglas toyed with nail polishes and lip-glosses. As a young woman, she studied accounting at Florida International University. She honed her sales skills as a representative for Kohler, the manufacturer of upscale plumbing supplies such as the golden faucets one might see in trendy nightspots or palatial manors.

Calling it divine intervention might be a stretch, but Duverglas did find her calling. "It wasn't that long ago that I was having a hard time finding my makeup in the right shades," the thirty-something entrepreneur told NiaOnline. "It was frustrating and time consuming. I knew there had to be a better way for us to get our beauty products." She decided to open a beauty business.

But instead of opening a local store where she would be selling products only to customers in the Miami area, Duverglas went straight into cyberspace. Her cosmetics website became a seller of sister-friendly cosmetics lines, including Black Opal, Iman, Flori Roberts, and Patti LaBelle.

Duverglas is just one of many sisters who have followed their passions by starting businesses. Businesses owned by women of color reached more than 1 million in 2002—or 20 percent of all majority-owned, privately held, women-owned firms in the country. That same year, there were some 365,110 firms owned by black women in the U.S., an increase of 16.7 percent since 1997.

Women cite a variety of reasons for starting a business, including the desire to achieve more independence and flexibility, to balance work and family more effectively, or to go around the predominantly male power structure to become CEO. "You don't want to waste your productive years working for someone else if it isn't what you *really* want your life to be about," advises career guru Walt F. J. Goodridge, author of *Turn Your Passion Into Profit: Information, Inspiration and Ideas to Help You Make Money Doing What You Love.*

Maybe you hate your job. Or maybe you love your job but simply want to earn some extra money. Perhaps you already have a product you want to bring to market. Or you want to start a home-based business so that you can spend more time with your children. Whatever the reason, you can find personal fulfillment by discovering your true passion and turning it into a business. Here's how.

Truth be told, starting your own business is one of the scariest things you can do. Most folks go without an insurance or retirement plan, a salary, or vacation during the startup phase of a company. Even after the business gets off the ground, the market for your product or service can change at any time.

Any aspiring sister CEO ought to consider the following:

• **Look at what you are good at and what you love to do.** The best business ideas usually come from people who worked in a certain industry and decided to start a business in that field or spin off a business in another segment of that market. Take into account your interests, abilities, and experience.

Interior designer Sheila Bridges always had an interest in art history, architecture, antiques, and furniture. "These are things I felt very passionate about, and I spent a lot of time looking at these things on the weekends," says Bridges, who started out working in the fashion industry as a retail buyer after graduating from Brown University.

Three years later she decided to switch careers and landed a position as an interior design assistant at a New York architectural firm. Because the company had only about ten employees, Bridges did virtually everything, including shopping for furniture and fabric, sitting in on client presentations, and handling billing and client correspondence. "It gave me the tools I eventually needed to start my own business [in 1994]," says the principal of a namesake firm. Bridges also holds a degree from the Parsons School of Design and studied decorative arts at Polimoda in Florence, Italy.

• **Start out part-time or develop a freelance relationship.** This may be your best bet if you don't have the savings to last the "winter" of the business. It should allow you to hold on to insurance, a salary, and some vacation time. Once the business is established, then you can go into it full-time.

Before she quit her regular gig, Bridges did freelance

work on the side. By the time she decided to work for herself, she had two sizable jobs with which she could support herself. "I figured that if it didn't work out, I could always go back to work for someone else," she says.

Today her clients include entertainers, entrepreneurs, and business professionals, ranging from Bad Boy's Sean Combs to former U.S. president Bill Clinton. Looking to tap Generation X and Y audiences, she authored *Furnishing Forward: A Practical Guide to Furnishing for a Lifetime*, an informative guide for young people.

• **Know your market.** The best way to become familiar with your market is to talk to potential customers, competitors, and suppliers. The key to your success will be how well you get to know your customers—their likes, dislikes, and buying patterns.

PART 5

REINVENTING YOURSELF

15

INTERVIEW

How Claire Huxtable Made it Look Easy
and Other Observations

FROM ACTRESS AND MOTHER PHYLICIA RASHAD

If the notion of happily "having it all" seems a bit fictitious at times, then no fictional character portrayed that ideal better than Claire Huxtable of television's *The Cosby Show* (1984–1992). She was a successful attorney, a loving mother of five active children, and the beautiful wife of an adoring and lovable OB-GYN, Cliff Huxtable (played by comedian Bill Cosby). Late child-support checks, missed recitals, looming deadlines, dust bunnies, the other woman, and stretch marks didn't exist in Claire's world. As we juggle the many balls that make up our real-world lives, it's tempting to ask, "Has any sister really lived such a perfect life? How did she make it all look so easy?"

"It's easy when you're scripted, the children are scripted, and the husband is scripted," recalls actress Phylicia Rashad, who played Claire. After pausing to laugh, she adds, "But I'm glad it serves as a source of inspiration for people."

As a three-times-divorced mother of two, Rashad is more

like the rest of us than her character, Claire. At the same time, she's exceptional. After several successful decades in show business, the fifty-six-year-old actress made history by being the first African American woman to win a Tony Award as a dramatic lead. She received it for her portrayal of matriarch Lena Younger in the 2004 Broadway revival of Lorraine Hansberry's *A Raisin in the Sun*.

Who better to discuss the challenges of balancing a fulfilling family life with a successful career? She shared her thoughts on being a "Cosby" mom; on how an early sacrifice aided the performing career of sister Debbie Allen, showing her what really mattered; and on enjoying life's simple pleasures.

What are the challenges of being a mother and pursuing a successful career?

During my pregnancy with my first son Billy, I received a call from a Broadway producer about a show, *Raisin*, a musical. I was being offered the role of Beneatha. And I thanked him for that call, but I told him I was great with child, and I couldn't possibly do it, but I did have a sister that I thought that they should see. They hired my sister Debbie to dance in the chorus, and they let her understudy that role, and when the actress that was playing that role decided to get very lovely one day, and prove her point by not showing up, Debbie went on and she was so fabulous that they told that other actress, "Well, you don't have to come back."

Three months after my son was born, the show was opening on Broadway [in 1973]. My mother came to visit. I wasn't working at all at the time. I was home being a mother. She held my son in her arms and she looked at me, and she said, "Phylicia, I know you think you're behind, but you're not. You are ahead." She looked at my son, and she looked at me, and she said, "You

will never do anything more important than this," and that is
the truth. I have never done anything more important than
rear my children.

But for me, that is the first and most important understanding. And with that understanding, my children are part of what
I do. They're not separate from it. It isn't that I've had my career on the left side of my life and my children on the right, or
vice versa. My children are very much a part of it.

**How did you integrate your children into the other parts of your
life?**

The first thing is to understand that you'll never do anything
greater than this, than to rear your children. And with that understanding your children are very much a part of everything
that you do. Immediately after I became a mother, I noticed
that I was a better actress. Immediately I noticed that my voice
was better, all because I was a mother. I felt beautiful for the
first time. And being a mother is very demanding. It doesn't
ever change. Oh, it shifts a little, yes, it takes on different fla-
vors, but it is really demanding, because it adds a lot of responsibilities, for life. And you can make it a joyful thing—it all de-
pends on your attitude and your own understanding.

How about balancing your life in relation to having a partner?

Well, now that gets to be another color. [Laughs] You know, you
don't have a child by yourself. So hopefully, that person is there
with that same joy, that same understanding, that same goal,
that same wanting "to be a part" of it all, and wanting to share.

It shouldn't become such a mental exercise, balancing your
life. I think there's something very debilitating about that. For
centuries people have had children and reared them very well,
without books, without "how-to" articles, without group discussion. But we have changed. We like to complicate things and

make them seem hard, and maybe because we think that gives them meaning, I don't know.

Claire Huxtable seemed to make it look so easy. She was an icon that a lot of women have looked to when trying to "have it all." I like to think of *The Cosby Show* as a beautiful picture of what realistically can and should be. And if you look really deeply into that series and into those people, you see that what made those relationships possible was a real respect between the man and the woman. A man who rejoiced in his wife's intellect, as well as her beauty. Here was a woman who knew that her husband stood by her all the time. And they had *fun*. Even when they disagreed, they had fun. And they worked to build a life *together*.

How do you take care of yourself?
Well, I take care of my skin every day. I like to eat very healthy foods—I like to eat organic foods. There're certain things I don't do: I don't drink alcoholic beverages and I don't smoke cigarettes, and I don't keep company with people who are unhappy. I just don't do it. That kind of stuff rubs off on you.

Is there a spiritual element to your life?
There's a spiritual element to all life. It just is.

We read that you do yoga.
People always say that. If you say, "I like to rise in the morning and sit quietly and become very still," the next thing you know, someone says, "You do yoga." And when people read, "She does yoga," then in their minds, it is not understood that all you said was that you like to sit quietly. They think, "Oh, she's doing those positions and she's got her legs up on the wall, and she's twisted like a pretzel." But I have studied Hatha yoga and I do enjoy that.

I like to be quiet. I like to sit quietly. I like to listen to gospel music and all forms of music that inspire a great inner feeling. I like to read books that I find inspiring. And when I say an inspiring book, I'm not just talking about a religious book, I'm talking about a book that is well written. Just the other day I picked up Thomas Hardy's *Far from the Madding Crowd.* Oh, I love this man's writing!

I like to go to museums and look at works of art, because now when I look at a work of art, I'm not just looking at what's on the canvas, or what's been shaped or molded. I'm looking to see what that artist was thinking about. "Hmmm, how did they come up with that?" And it's so amazing because you see the potential of a human being. You see the potential of the human mind and creative spirit, and that's inspiring.

And you know what I really like? I love to sit out in nature. Oh, I like that best of all. To go to the botanical gardens and sit, or to sit in my own garden, or to find a beautiful spot near a river, I like that a lot. I like to watch the birds in August and early September as they begin practicing for their flights, when the weather's going to change. I like to watch the geese fly, too. I like those things. And I like to watch my cat's behavior. I like these things. And I like to sit in places sometimes where I can hear children laughing.

16

The Hot New Trend
for **Women:**

REINVENTING OURSELVES

Whether it happens around the thirtieth birthday or the fiftieth, at some point most women realize that life is short, so you might as well go for your goals.

Mothers are incredibly creative. They can make soup out of a turkey carcass. On single-parent salaries, some moms even figure out ways to pay for their children's college educations. But one of the most rewarding things any woman—whether a mother or not—can do is to use that determination to create her own "before and after."

Inventing ourselves time and again, making a way out of no way, going where there is no map, doing the unexpected and still coming out on top make all of us "mothers of reinvention." Read on to learn the stories of some inspiring women who have followed their purpose and passion, and find out who is the country's most famous reinvented mama of them all.

From Personnel Manager to Designing Woman

On the left coast, Susan Long-Walsh has reinvented herself lots of times. A mother of three, this sister in her forties has worked at all the hot Seattle companies, including Microsoft, Nordstrom, and Starbucks. But a few years ago, Long-Walsh quit her high-pressure job as a staffing manager in the human resources department of Microsoft cofounder Paul Allen's company, Vulcan, for a more laid-back job as an interior designer with the Ethan Allen home-furnishings company.

"I get to use my creative side and my ability to work well with people. I feel like a new person," Long-Walsh said after making the move. "So many women say to me, 'You are so lucky, girl!' Their comments have made me realize how many women are in jobs that don't make them happy. I just wanted to be as happy at work as I was when I came home."

Choosing Pound Cake over Hair Care

Amy Hilliard is a mother of reinvention too. Formerly employed at L'Oreal as senior vice president of marketing for Soft Sheen Products, she took the plunge a few years ago to start her own gourmet pound-cake company. ComfortCake, headquartered in Chicago, manufactures and distributes gourmet pound cakes worldwide to food-service accounts such as United Airlines and the Chicago Public Schools, retailers, and other customers on the web.

"Reinventing myself from a corporate executive to an entrepreneur this time feels more like letting my real self blossom," says the single mom of two. "I've always loved making and marketing products, and now I'm doing it for myself and my family. I feel more comfortable, secure, and empowered than I've ever felt before, even though having my own business is risky. The ability to chart my own course is the most reward-ing feeling. And letting my teenagers see that it can be done is vital because it shows what options are out there if you are pre-pared, and that obstacles can be overcome."

The Premier Mother of Reinvention...

And the most famous reinvented mama of them all? (Drum roll, please.) It's Hillary Clinton. Reinventing herself by dar-ing to run for the Senate, she made history by becoming the first First Lady to become a member of Congress. With her one child graduating from college, she decided not to sit home and twiddle her thumbs after her husband stepped down from the presidency. It took some guts to break the mold.

Following your purpose by reinventing yourself is not an easy thing to do. It takes planning, budgeting, emotional support, and tenacity. Initially, if you strike out solo, you may make less money than you did before, but you may also find that it feels like "positive poverty." When you're moving in an upward direction, your peace of mind is worth more than money.

More and more women are finding that out. There's a self-help book out on the art of "serial reinvention" by Candace Carpenter, the former CEO and cofounder of the women's web-site iVillage, who later decided to be—guess what?—a housewife. *Chapters: Create a Life of Exhilaration and Accomplishment in the Face of Change* tells how to go from unemployed to reinvented. You can do it too!

17

SHE'S PREACHING
the Gospel of Money

Several years ago, the Reverend James Meeks—the pastor of Salem Baptist Church, Chicago's largest African American church—asked his congregation how many of them were in debt.

Everyone raised a hand.

It was at that point that the church came up with a plan for how members could get out of debt. The stated goal for everyone? To become debt-free by 2003.

Three years into the plan, the church started receiving reports that many of the members had made drastic improvements in their debt situations. Rev. Meeks decided to introduce the members to the fundamentals of investing.

It's certainly an area in which too many of us have fallen behind. African Americans make up 12.7 percent of the United States' total population but account for only 2 percent of this country's wealth. Rev. Meeks created a new department, Financial Ministries, and hired Bonita Parker to be director of investment and economic empowerment.

Parker had come to Salem after fourteen years at Northern Trust Bank, where she attained the position of second vice president. "The more we learn about money management, the more our values will begin to change," Parker said. She was appointed national director of the Rainbow/PUSH Coalition's 1,000 Churches Connected to help spread the word of economic empowerment. "So the name-brand shoes that you bought a few years ago won't mean as much today as when you were more frivolous with your spending."

For as long as she can remember, Parker said, she has been interested in money. But it is only in recent years that she has learned the value of investing and passing the knowledge on to others: "My first job out of college was at a bank. One of my white colleagues was the same age I was. We had the same level of academic accomplishments, and we had been working at the bank the same amount of time, but he knew much more than I did about finances and the markets. One day he asked me, 'At dinner, what does your family talk about?' "

One of seven children, Parker told him that it was rare for the whole family to sit down to meals together. But when they did, they talked mainly about church. "My family had dinner together every night," she said. "And we also talked about economics, how the market was doing, the prime rate, and investments. I realized then that my family had access to capital. We just didn't know what to do with it."

Eventually Parker's family began running an investment club, Saving by Grace, that met every month to discuss the stock market.

Since coming to Salem Baptist Church, Parker has helped

introduce the congregation to classes on saving, investing, and home buying. Altogether, some 125 financial clubs have been formed at the church, each with an average of ten members. Reflecting the congregation's makeup, most club members are in their thirties or forties. A workshop on investment clubs has been especially successful: "For seven consecutive Monday nights, we had roughly 1,200 people attend classes on investing. The first couple of weeks, we addressed setting up an investment club, while the rest of the training dealt with areas such as how to research stocks. We graduated well over 850 people from those sessions. We encouraged them to reach out to family members and friends to form their own investment clubs."

In presenting her own financial wisdom, Parker refers to a series of sermons by Rev. Meeks in which he points to several biblical references that deal with material possessions and the correct use of money. One of his favorites is the story of the talents, in Matthew 25: 14-30. A traditional interpretation of the talents has been to use all of God's gifts and blessings. But Parker said the pastor has shown that Jesus was teaching us what to do with money.

18

EMPOWERMENT

Straight

from the Hood

Just over a decade ago, students from Crenshaw High School in Los Angeles decided to do their part to rebuild one of the areas hardest hit by the 1992 riots. The teens restored a weed-infested vegetable garden behind their school's football field.

The students' efforts quickly took root, and with the assistance of their science teacher and a local businesswoman, the student-owned business Food From the Hood was born. In 1993 the business began to market a salad dressing in addition to growing and selling produce.

But Food From the Hood is about more than entrepreneurship: it also enables students to log hours and receive compensation in the form of direct scholarships to a post-secondary trade school, college, or university. Fifty percent of profits from salad-dressing sales go into the scholarship fund. The other half is reinvested in the business. As of 2002, some seventy-seven Crenshaw graduates had received nearly $200,000 in scholarship money.

Monique Hunter became involved with the youth program in 1999. She became the group's executive director, and took the lead in helping Food From the Hood continue to thrive. In 2002 she spoke with NiaOnline about her involvement. Her profile illustrates how it's possible to reapply your skill set to gain greater fulfillment in life, and help a younger generation.

An engineer by training, Hunter, spent fourteen years in corporate America before starting a travel-and-events–planning firm: "I always had that entrepreneurial spirit, whether it was teaching kids how to start businesses or running my own. I started my business because I was looking for something that was going to be fun, that I could enter on the ground level and build quickly, and that I could run from home."

Hunter's business, Unity Travel, blossomed into a 1,200-square-foot facility and co-op made up of several other small businesses. She left the business after her husband's sudden death in 1998.

Around that time, the chairman of the science department at Crenshaw High School—also an African American woman who had decided to leave corporate America—invited Hunter to serve as a professional expert at the school. Her role was to identify and train students in laboratory techniques and set up lab experiments. "I met one of the cofounders of Food From the Hood on a trip to Africa," she recalled. "I told her I was working with these kids from Crenshaw in science and she said, 'You should meet the executive director of Food From the Hood.' Even though I knew about the group, I had never gone to the back of the school to see the garden."

She met with the executive director at the time, Aleyne Larner. Hunter was impressed with the students' green thumbs but realized that they needed more marketing savvy. She started working with the kids on a volunteer basis, teaching them about writing a business plan and promoting the salad dressing.

Shortly afterward she became chair of the group's board of directors, and in 2001 she took the reins as executive director. Part of the new direction of Food From the Hood was to reestablish a presence in southern California, to create "sister schools," and to get alumni and board members working with the students. "One thing I learned when my husband suddenly left the planet is that we really do not have a firm financial base. We also don't understand how money works or how to invest it," she said.

"I started an investment club for women and passed that financial knowledge on to the students. Before, they would get scholarship money that sat in a regular bank account until they went to college. Now those dollars are invested in a 529 College Savings Plan, where students get to monitor their individual funds and watch them grow."

Hunter continued to work to empower women. While watching Los Angeles burn during the 1992 upheaval, she and her friends decided that they needed a vehicle to inspire and expand their lives. They formed a book club, focusing on how-to books about finance and economics, as well as health and race relations.

Hunter's motivation is simple: "At this point, I am all about empowerment in my personal and professional life."

19

From Civil Servant *to* Massage Therapist

Deneen McReynolds quit her government job to master the art of healing through massage, Reiki, and stone therapy.

She attended Clark Atlanta University with aspirations of being a news anchor. But she soon realized that she didn't have what it took to be an in-your-face reporter.

After graduating in 1987, she spent the next ten years working in civil service, including a stint as program coordinator for the New Jersey State Department of Housing and Community Development. She even had a short gig as press secretary for the mayor of Orange, New Jersey. In 1999 she decided to pack up and move to Washington DC. Having worked in municipal and state government, she figured her next logical step was to work at the federal level.

But McReynolds had trouble finding the right job, so she decided to explore a longtime interest: massage therapy. Taking

$5,000 in savings, she applied to the Virginia Learning Institute, where she then spent six months taking 500 hours' worth of courses on anatomy, biology, and physiology. She studied every aspect of the body—from muscles and bones to nerves and layers of the skin. McReynolds also studied advanced Reiki (healing through touch), and eventually became a certified Reiki practitioner. The two therapeutic practices seemed like a natural fit.

After finishing school, McReynolds landed her dream government job with a national contractor for the U.S. Department of Housing and Urban Development. But the free spirit still managed to put her newfound training to good use by working weekends at a local health club and spa.

Soon, however, the travel required by her full-time job began to interfere with her part-time work. After a year and four months of civil duty, she decided to call it quits and to pursue what she believed to be her divine purpose in life. "I believe that everybody has been created to actualize his or her divine purpose," she said. "Part of that fabric for me is to be of service and to work in concert with the universe as a healer and a writer. I feel that massage is a way to aid in our general wellness and to bring balance to our hectic lives."

How do you feel about your job?	
I love it	24%
I like it somewhat	29%
I neither like nor dislike it	17%
I dislike it somewhat	14%
I hate it!	9%
I don't know	7%

McReynolds had first become interested in massage therapy in 1996. The self-taught masseuse read books on the subject and practiced on friends and relatives. She took a summer course at the Kinetic Institute in New Jersey and later recalled the burgeoning importance of her newly full-time profession: "As part of a research project, I learned that ancient Egyptians used massage for healing. My interest came out of wanting to know more about that aspect. At the same time, I noticed that message therapy was becoming more prevalent and that insurance companies were starting to pay for it."

As a therapist, McReynolds was paid $10 an hour plus commission and tips, a far cry from her $50,000 annual salary (plus a pension) as a civil service worker. She came to average between two and six clients a day. In addition to massage and Reiki, she also performed stone therapy—mastered through on-the-job training.

"Massage is the manipulation of soft tissue and the stimulation of blood flow and oxygen to the cells," she explains. "Reiki is a 'laying of hands'—kept slightly elevated over the body—on chakras, or the body's energy centers. Stone therapy involves taking stones from quarries, using their thermal properties (they are heated to 128 degrees), and placing them on certain parts of the body—such as palms of the hand, or the feet, chest, or back—for energetic or healing purposes.

"I believe everybody has the power to heal him- or herself. You see older women put their hands on their hips. Sometimes when we do that we are giving ourselves our own energy; we are giving healing to ourselves."

The "old sage," as she describes herself, has always gravitated toward natural healing. She uses homeopathic remedies in much the same way as many of our grandmothers. While as a strict vegetarian she eats well, being a therapist has taken its toll on her body.

"This is very physical work. It involves a lot of wear and tear on your joints, fingers, thumbs, and legs. I started to get varicose veins. This experience has prompted me to get in shape physically. I do yoga now and stretching, which is so essential. In this job, you need to be light on your feet."

20

IF AT FIRST YOU
Don't Succeed,
Try Again

Clara Villarosa has worn several hats. She has been a social worker, an assistant hospital administrator, and the vice president of a bank. For nearly two decades, however, she has been one of the country's most respected booksellers.

Villarosa, who ran a prominent bookstore in Denver (a city of about 100,000 African Americans), moved in 2000 to New York City's Harlem, which has some 600,000 black residents. November 2001 marked the grand opening of the Hue-Man Bookstore, which is part of "Harlem USA," a federally designated "empowerment zone."

Since 1992, Harlem USA officials had been trying to get other booksellers to set up shop—namely, Barnes & Noble and Borders—but were turned down. Neighboring businesses include Disney, Magic Johnson theaters, Old Navy, and J.P Morgan Chase Bank. Hue-Man also sits two and a half blocks from the office of former President Bill Clinton, who began

Have you ever dreamed of owning your own business or being self-employed?

Yes	90%
No	10%

the enormous book tour to promote his autobiography by appearing first at Hue-Man.

Her road to success, however, has not been easy. In fact, her first business venture failed. Here, Villarosa shares her personal experience and advice on how to bounce back from failure and take that first step in following your passion—whether it's starting a business or going back to school. "I had decided to start a consulting business. I was going to consult with corporations to help them with diversity. This was in the late 1970s and early '80s, so this concept was way before its time.

"Over a period of six months, I hit the streets and left my resume. It was hard to get my foot in the door. I didn't have a clue how to go about it—you can't just knock on corporate doors with a business card and a little brochure. I never got to the point where I had any clients."

Villarosa admitted she didn't have a game plan. And subsequently, the business failed. But just because the business failed doesn't mean she was a failure. It meant only that she wasn't prepared. She was determined to do a better job the second time around: "I learned from the experience. I realized that I didn't have enough background to sell a service. I decided that with the next business I started, I would sell a concrete product instead of trying to sell myself. I needed to identify a product and develop a business plan around that product."

She came up with the criteria for her product: one, it must be a product she had a passion for; and two, it must relate to black people. She decided on an African American bookstore, since she was an avid reader with a passion for books.

She learned about courses offered through the Small Business Development Centers and the Service Corps of Retired

Executives (SCORE). In order to learn about the retail business, she took one-day seminars on how to start a business, write a business plan, and tackle taxes and accounting matters. Still, the business didn't generate a lot of sales that first year. "I didn't understand the market," she said. "I had based my research on general bookstores. But I had an African American bookstore, which is a specialty store. I wasn't necessarily selling books, but rather culture. I had to concentrate on customers who were going to be more culturally connected.

"First I identified who came into the store. It was not the people I had marketed to—the middle class who had disposable income to buy books. I realized that it was working-class people who were coming into the store. In order to reach out to them, I extended my marketing strategies to churches. I also realized that the middle class people really valued "the best"— they were very much conspicuous consumers. So I started marketing my store as the largest black bookstore in the country, in order to motivate them to come into the store."

It took about five years for Villarosa to break even (so that gross profits equaled fixed costs). The business began to grow, with a 15 percent annual increase in sales. One key to Villarosa's success: branding. She has become an authority on issues pertaining to black books and publishing. She is the first black woman to serve on the American Booksellers Association board of directors. She also founded the American Black Booksellers Association.

Having run a smaller bookstore for more than a decade, Villarosa has the experience needed to make the newest Hue-Man Bookstore a Harlem success story. But there's one more essential ingredient that gives her the strength and confidence to take on a project of such magnitude: "I have faith in God and in myself."

21

ONE SISTER'S JOURNEY TO

Becoming
a Writer

Sarah Greaves-Gabbadon spent five months in New York City working as an unpaid intern at a women's health-and-fitness magazine. She had the time of her life, reveling in the frenetic pace of the Big Apple, the company of new friends, and most of all, work in a field she found stimulating.

After returning to her corporate job in Montego Bay, Jamaica, the public relations executive found that she wasn't excited about being back at the office. All she felt was dread and a persistent knot in the pit of her stomach. By the end of that first week, she knew she had to make a change: "Although I still enjoyed the work itself, the machinations and jockeying for position that surrounded me—which I'd previously found vaguely amusing—now drained and disgusted me. While nothing at the company had changed in my absence," she notes, "I knew that I had. I also knew that if I stayed, my choices were limited; I could either swim with the sharks, become one myself, or be eaten alive. I chose to get out of the water."

A few months later, Greaves-Gabbadon resigned, to the surprise of colleagues and the bewilderment of friends and family. She had everything she had been raised to believe was a hallmark of professional success: a high-profile, much-coveted job; a handsome salary; a home; and first-class business travel (in the company jet). Despite such riches, she longed to express a more creative side.

"For six months I tried tirelessly to get a full-time writing position on a London magazine," she recalled about her first efforts, in a 2001 interview with NiaOnline. "Even my offers to volunteer were politely declined. I found a part-time job in a bookstore, to cover basic living expenses. I worked for just a month before I was fired. (The person I had replaced had a change of heart and returned to work.) The only work I did in those six months was an article about "hip, cool" London, commissioned by a Jamaican magazine. I was disappointed, scared, and humbled. I resolved to return to Jamaica."

Greaves-Gabbadon had leased her apartment, so after fifteen years of flying solo, she moved back home with her parents. Coincidentally, the same Jamaican editor who had commissioned the London article started assigning a small but steady supply of stories. The following year, Greaves-Gabbadon moved back into her apartment. She later landed an assignment to review a resort in Barbados. Since then, she has written more than sixty published articles. Her work appears on the web and in local newspapers and international magazines.

What is your current job status?	
Employed	72%
Full-time student	6%
Homemaker	7%
Self-employed or business owner	6%
Unemployed	9%

She reflected on her current situation and how her life's circumstances have changed in reaching that point: "Today I have a new and authentic identity as a writer. I'm doing the work I know I was born to do. Yes, money is tight (I now earn less than half my corporate salary), and my credit cards balances aren't always paid in full. Living without financial security is scary, and I still have moments of self-doubt, though they're fewer and more fleeting. I am immensely grateful for the opportunity to do what I love. I'm living my life by design, not by default, plotting my path and creating my own happy ending. And believe me, that means so much more than a ride in the corporate jet."

RESOURCE GUIDE

ORGANIZING RESOURCES

National Association of Professional Organizers
Description: This nonprofit offers a free, national online locator of professional organizers in a variety of specialties, including time management, closet organizing, feng shui, and more.
Address: 4700 West Lake Avenue, Glenview, IL 60025
Phone: 847-375-4746
Web: http://www.napo.net

Get It Together: Home, Office & Estate Organization
Description: This service offers professional assistance in organizing and maintaining an ordered office, home, or any other space.
Address: 172 Fifth Avenue, Suite 252, Brooklyn, NY 11217
Phone: 718-783-2077
Fax: 718-783-7772
Email: staff@getit-together.com
Web: http://www.getit-together.com

The Container Store
Description: One-stop-shopping for home and office organization and storage.
Address: Nationwide (Check the website or call for locations)
Phone: 888-CONTAIN (888-266-8246)
Web: http://www.containerstore.com

TIME-SAVING RESOURCES

International Concierge and Errand Association
Description: The USA Membership Directory of this worldwide organization lists professionals who provide concierge, errand, and personal assistant services.
Address: 4932 Castor Avenue, Philadelphia, PA 19124
Phone: 215-743-5618
Email: info@iceaweb.org
Web: http://www.iceaweb.org

Hire-A-Chef
Description: Hireachef.com provides an online locator connecting people with affordable personal chef services in their area. Services are generally provided in your own home, with up to two week's worth of meals prepared at a time. It is sponsored by the United States Personal Chef Association and the Canadian Personal Chef Association.
Phone: 800-995-2138
Web: http://www.hireachef.com

American Personal Chef Association
Description: This professional organization provides a national online directory of personal chefs.
Address: 4572 Delaware Street, San Diego, CA 92116
Phone: 800-644-8389
Email: info@personalchef.com
Web: http://www.personalchefsearch.com

Fresh Direct

Description: Grocery delivery to certain neighborhoods in New York, including Manhattan, Brooklyn, and Queens.

Phone: 866-283-7374

Web: http://www.freshdirect.com

Service Master

Description: ServiceMaster's subsidiary companies provide home cleaning, lawn care, home maintenance, and pest control services under brand names such as ChemLawn, Terminix, and Merry Maids. Use their website to obtain consultations and referrals to services in your area.

Address: 3250 Lacey Road, Suite 600, Downers Grove, IL 60515

Phone: 866-937-3783

Email: customercare@servicemaster.com

Web: http://www.servicemaster.com

STRESS REDUCTION RESOURCES

Cynergy New York Spa and Wellness Center

Description: Owned by Cynthia Grace, a clinical psychologist, New York-based Cynergy has a location in Harlem and one in Brooklyn. Its signature services include an Ancestral Aromatherapy Massage, a therapeutic homage to Africa.

Phone: 212-491-7880 or 718-403-9242

Web: http://www.cynergyspa.com/

Power Living Enterprises, Inc.

Description: A Harlem-based company dedicated to helping people from all walks of life to live better lives. Its services include lifestyle coaching and yoga classes.

Address: 71 West 128th Street, Third Floor, Suite B, New York, NY 10027

Phone: 212-289-6363 or 212-348-1218

Email: info@power-living.com

Web: http://www.power-living.com

International Spa Association
Description: This professional organization says it represents over 2,000 wellness facilities. Its website includes a national spa locator.
Address: 2365 Harrodsburg Road, Suite A325, Lexington, KY 40504
Phone: 859-226-4326 or 888-651-4772
Web: http://www.experienceispa.com/

Spa Finder
Description: Spa Finder provides information about day spas, vacation spas, and medical spas around the world. Its website includes a spa locator.
Address: 91 Fifth Avenue, Sixth Floor, New York, NY 10003
Phone: 212-924-6800
Web: http://www.spafinder.com

Health Club Locator
Description: Provided by the American Council on Exercise, this is a handy resource to find a health club in your area.
Address: 4851 Paramount Drive, San Diego, CA 92123
Phone: 800-825-3636
Web: http://www.acefitness.org/clublocator

Voice of Dance
Description: Sponsored in part by Danskin, this comprehensive dance-related resource's website provides information for taking local dance lessons and has a global directory of over 25,000 dance-related companies and organizations. Use it to find classes in African and Brazilian-style dancing, capoeira, jazz movement, salsa, and more.
Address: 850 College Avenue, Kentfield, CA 94904
Phone: 415-460-5150
Email: info@voiceofdance.com
Web: http://www.voiceofdance.com/Classes/ClassMain.cfm

COUNSELING AND FAMILY SUPPORT RESOURCES

National Mental Health Consumers' Self-Help Clearinghouse
Description: Provides the public with information about materials and resources concerning mental health issues, including stress.
Address: 1211 Chestnut Street, Suite 1207, Philadelphia, PA 19107
Phone: 800-553-4539 or 215-751-1810
Email: info@mhselfhelp,org
Web: http://www.mhselfhelp.org

National Women's Health Information Center
Description: A U.S. federal government clearinghouse of information about women's health issues, including stress.
Address: 8550 Arlington Boulevard, Suite 300, Fairfax, VA 22031
Phone: 800-994-9662 or 888-220-5446
Web: http://www.4woman.gov

National Mental Health Association
Description: Find a therapist, psychologist, psychiatrist, social worker, or counselor using this nonprofit's online locator.
Address: 2001 North Beauregard Street, Twelfth Floor, Alexandria, Virginia 22311
Phone: 800-969-6642
Web: http://www.nmha.org

Families and Work Institute
Description: Learn more about trends in the balance between work and home life via the Families and Work Institute.
Address: 267 Fifth Avenue, Second Floor, New York, NY 10016
Phone: 212-465-2044
Web: http://www.familiesandwork.org

Family Support America

Description: A nationwide database of family support programs and family support practitioners across the country. Check out the Family Support Mapping Project for information about programs and resources in your area.

Address: 205 West Randolph Street, Suite 2222, Chicago, IL 60606

Phone: 312-338-0900

Web: http://www.familysupportamerica.org

SUPPORT RESOURCES FOR PARENTS AND CAREGIVERS

Childcare Aware

Description: Childcare Aware provides parents with information about childcare and referrals to local providers.

Address: 1319 F Street NW, Suite 500, Washington, DC 20004

Phone: 800-424-2246

Email: info@childcareaware.org

Web: http://www.childcareaware.org

Big Brothers Big Sisters of America

Description: A great source of support for single parents, Big Brothers Big Sisters aims to help children reach their potential through professionally supported, one-to-one mentoring relationships.

Address: National Office, 230 North Thirteenth Street,
           Philadelphia, PA 19107

Phone: 215-567-7000

Web: http://www.bbbsa.org

Mocha Moms

Description: Mocha Moms is a support group for mothers of color who have chosen not to work full-time outside of the home in order to devote more time to their families.

Address: National Office, P.O. Box 1995, Upper Marlboro, MD 20773

Email: membership@mochamoms.org

Web: http://www.mochamoms.org

Eldercare Locator

Description: The Eldercare Locator connects older Americans and their caregivers with sources of information on senior services.
Phone: 800-677-1116
Email: eldercare_locator@aoa.gov
Web: http://www.eldercare.gov/Eldercare/Public/Home.asp

BUSINESS STARTUP RESOURCES

Association for Enterprise Opportunity

Description: Offers financial assistance, training, and technical assistance, as well as a menu of services for startup companies.
Address: 1601 North Kent, Suite 1101, Arlington, VA 22209
Phone: 703-841-7748
Email: aeo@assoceo.org
Web: http://www.microenterpriseworks.org

National Association of Women Business Owners

Description: Offers information resources, advocacy, member discounts for business equipment and services, and financial products and services through alliance partners.
Address: 1411 K Street NW, Suite 1300, Washington, DC 20005
Phone: 202-347-8686
Email: national@nawbo.org
Web: http://www.nawbo.org

The National Black Chamber of Commerce

Description: Offers procurement opportunities, technical assistance, and e-commerce.
Address: 1350 Connecticut Avenue NW, Suite 825,
        Washington, DC 20036
Phone: 202-466-6888
Email: info@nationalbcc.org
Web: http://www.nationalbcc.org

Office of Women's Business Ownership

Description: Offers business training, technical assistance, access to credit and capital, federal contracts, and international trade opportunities.
Address: 409 Third Street NW, Fourth Floor, Washington, DC 20416
Phone: 202-205-6673
Email: owbo@sba.gov
Web: http://www.sba.gov/ed/wbo/index.html

Count-Me-In

Description: Nonprofit organization that provides access to business loans, consultation, and education, as well as access to networks that expand contacts, markets, and skills.
Address: 240 Central Park South, Suite 7H, New York, NY 10019
Phone: 212-245-1245
Email: info@count-me-in.org
Web: http://www.count-me-in.org

The American Woman's Economic Development Corporation

Description: Offers training and counseling for women at all levels, from startups to million-dollar enterprises.
Address: 216 East 45th Street, Tenth Floor, New York, NY 10017
Phone: 917-368-6100
Email: info@awed.org
Web: http://www.awed.org

Business.gov

Description: This online government information portal promises to "guide you through the maze of government rules and regulations, and provide access to services and resources to help you start, grow, and succeed in business." It's a good place for basic business startup information.
Web: http://www.business.gov

United States Small Business Administration (SBA)
Description: The SBA assists with business startups, financing, administration, and more. Among other things, it guarantees certain small business loans. To locate the local district office in your state, use the locator map on the website's homepage.
Address: Headquarters Office, 409 Third Street, SW,
        Washington, DC 20416
Phone: 800-U-ASK-SBA
Web: http://www.sba.gov

Online Women's Business Center
Description: Sponsored by the SBA, this resource promotes the growth of women-owned businesses through programs that address business training and technical assistance, and provide access to credit and capital, federal contracts, and international trade opportunities.
Web: http://www.onlinewbc.gov

Women's Business Development Center
Description: The WBDC offers a full-service approach to launching emerging businesses and strengthening existing businesses owned by women in the Chicago area.
Address: 8 South Michigan Avenue, Suite 400, Chicago, IL 60603
Phone: 312-853-3477
Email: wbdc@wbdc.org

JOB SEARCH RESOURCES

Career OneStop
Description: This is your government gateway to job listings, resumes, and career information nationwide—a huge collection of free employment and career resources on the internet.
Phone: 877-348-0502
Email: career.onestop@state.mn.us
Web: http://www.careeronestop.org

Diversity Inc. Career Center

Description: DiversityInc's Career Center includes a job bank of positions at companies who are seeking a diverse workforce.
Address: 317 George Street, New Brunswick, NJ 08901
Phone: 732-509-5250
Email: info@diversityinc.com
Web: http://www.diversityinc.com/public/department33.cfm

Monster.com

Description: This major job search resource includes a database of companies that value "diversity and inclusion," as well as a section of career advice for African Americans.
Phone: 800-MONSTER
Web: http://diversity.monster.com/?opt=6

CareerBuilder.com

Description: Use one of the nation's largest employment networks to find jobs locally or nationally. Its website includes a page that lists companies seeking diversity.
Address: Corporate Headquarters, 8420 West Bryn Mawr Avenue,
        Suite 1000, Chicago, IL 60631
Phone: 866-438-1485
Web: http://www.careerbuilder.com/JobSeeker/Jobs/Diversity.htm

CAREER COACHES AND COUNSELORS

National Career Development Association

Description: The NCDA serves professionals in the career development field; however, its website features a directory search for finding a career counselor in your area, as well as what to look for in a career counselor.
Address: Headquarters: 10820 East 45th Street, Suite 210,
        Tulsa, OK 74146
Phone: 866-FOR-NCDA
Web: http://www.ncda.org/

International Coach Federation
Description: The ICF is a professional association for personal and business coaches. Its website includes a coaching referral service.
Address: 1444 "I" Street NW, Suite 700, Washington, DC 20005
Phone: 888-423-3131
Email: icfoffice@coachfederation.org
Web: http://www.coachfederation.org/referral

The Work Doctor and Associates
Description: Headed by career coach and author Daphne Houston, PhD (a.k.a. "The Work Doctor"), this company provides a variety of personal coaching services.
Address: 15455 North Dallas Parkway, Sixth Floor, Addison, TX 75001
Phone: 972-818-3939
Web: http://www.daphnehouston.com

The Journey Productions
Description: Headed by author and life coach Jennifer Lewis-Hall, this company provides personal coaching services for people seeking more satisfying careers.
Email: thejourneyproductions@msn.com
Web: http://www.jenniferlewishall.com

profundities
Description: Headed by life coach, author, and nationally-syndicated columnist Harriette Cole, profundities provides life coaching services to celebrities and the general public.
Address: 10 West 15th Street, Suite 526, New York, NY 10001
Phone: 212-645-3005
Web: http://www.harriettecole.com

READING LIST

The Nia Guide for Black Women: Achieving Career Success on Your Terms **(Agate, 2004)**
by Sheryl Huggins and Cheryl Mayberry McKissack

Daily Cornbread: 365 Secrets for a Healthy Mind, Body, and Spirit **(Doubleday, 1999)**
by Stephanie Stokes Oliver

Seven Soulful Secrets: For Finding Your Purpose and Minding Your Mission **(Harlem Moon, 2002)**
by Stephanie Stokes Oliver

Choosing Truth: Living an Authentic Life **(Simon & Schuster, 2003)**
by Harriette Cole

Having It All? Black Women and Success **(Doubleday, 2003)**
by Veronica Chambers

Having What Matters: The Black Woman's Guide to Creating the Life You Really Want (Amistad Press, 2002)
by Monique Greenwood

Life's a Journey—Not a Sprint: Navigating Life's Challenges and Finding Your Pathway to Success (Hay House, Inc., 2004)
by Jennifer Lewis-Hall

Practical Parenting (Mountain Movers Press, 2000)
by Montel Williams and Jeffrey Gardere, PhD

The Real Lives of Strong Black Women: Transcending Myths, Reclaiming Joy (Agate, 2004)
by Toby Thompkins